IF PAR

IS A THREE-RING CIRCUS,

HOW COME I'M NOT
THE RINGMASTER?

Creative Ways to Raise Great Kids!

by

TOM L. SANFORD

If Parenting is a Three Ring Circus
How Come I'm Not the Ringmaster?
© 2004, 2005 by Tom L. Sanford

ISBN: 0-936785-97-7

Design by Lastra & Associates
Back cover photo by Teresa Farnsworth

Published by The Concerned Group
Siloam Springs, AR   72761

Dedicated to

my wife, Bonnie,

and our two children,

Kelly and Craig

CONTENTS

ACKNOWLEDGEMENTS

I must, first and foremost, express my deep appreciation to my wife, Bonnie, who for years has encouraged me to write this book. And to my two wonderful children, Kelly and Craig, who played such an important role in encouraging me to think outside the box of traditional disciplining. It is true that most of the time they were oblivious of their involvement, but their participation indeed challenged me to be a better father. They have been so kind to let me share stories from their childhood.

Perhaps the greatest honor a writer can have is to have his own children write the preface and post script to validate the contents of the book.

Special acknowledgement must be made to all the young people whose stories I have shared and the volumes of stories that are left untold. The names have all been changed, and in some cases the details have been altered a bit to avoid recognition.

Many of the examples were of young people who have been residents at Project PATCH Ranch. (www.projectpatch.org)

PREFACE

March 1, 1970 marks the day I first met Tom Sanford. While I don't remember anything about our introduction, that date was to be the beginning of a life-long relationship. Tom was launched, headfirst, into the joys, sorrows, rewards and frustrations of parenting. And I was to be the first one to test his skills.

My dad grew up in a home void of nurturing love and filled with punitive punishment. So, from the beginning, he strove to raise his own children with love, respect, and creative discipline. I quickly became the *apple of his eye* and thrived under his unconditional love.

Using humor in tense parenting situations was to become my dad's survival technique. Whenever I was sick and had to take some "nasty, awful, terrible, it-will-kill-me" medicine my mom was doling out, my dad would follow it up with two M&Ms in a little paper cup with the instructions, "Take two and see me in the morning." Sometimes I would get the same *prescription* after an especially hard day (the kind you have in second grade) when I poured my heart out in sobs to his listening ear.

As I grew older, my dad made sure to include me in decisions that affected me. This respect, so often denied young children, showed me I was an important part of the family and that he cared about my input. I was allowed to give my opinion on new cars our family purchased (even if it was only the color). When a family move forced me to leave my treasured, customized tree house my dad built, I was allowed to negotiate a deal to *sell* it to the family who was buying our country home. This helped ease the pain of leaving and allowed me to dream about new adventures in a new home.

My dad believes in relevant and immediate consequences. Add this belief to his humor, and it was hard to stay one step ahead of him as a pre-teen. I would try little things to exert my independence and/or push some buttons. For several days in a row I would lean back in my chair at the table while I ate, something I knew wouldn't be acceptable. I let my parents' requests to sit up fall on deaf ears just to see what they would/could do about it. After a couple of days I felt like I was gaining ground and smugly threw myself back in the chair at breakfast only to find it wouldn't budge. I tried, casually, to survey the situation and found that the chair legs had been nailed to the floor. This action caught me by surprise and ultimately solved the problem without adding strain to my relationship with my parents.

Despite such caring and creativity, I still took the role of a first child and challenged the system. I remember telling my parents how angry I was that I could never run away from home. (At that time, all the run-aways in the county were housed at our home after being picked up by the police.) However, this angry outburst was defused when my dad said they would help me pack and ask the police to take me straight to jail instead of back home again. I remember missing my curfew deadline only to be told I should call if I was running late so they wouldn't worry. Growing up there were always boundaries and rules but those were enforced with love, respect and a little humor thrown in.

This is no ordinary parenting book. But, then again, the author isn't an ordinary parent. Since that day in 1970, my dad has been instrumental in the well-being and care of over 3,000 young people, including my brother and me. Tom Sanford has shown through his life, and in the pages of this book, just how timeless and necessary creative discipline is for a child.

Thanks, Dad, for the memories!

Kelly Sanford Hagele

INTRODUCTION

The family is the nucleus of civilization.

– ARIEL & WILL DURANT

Arise, O parents, and take back the empire that was snatched from your very grasp! The invading army is not a triumphal entry into your territory by outside forces. No, no. Rather, it is a subtle and almost imperceptible invasion by the *little people*. You know, your children whom you thought were so *cute* at one time and now are so obnoxious? It's not that their behavior has changed. That's the problem. They are behaving in the same manner that brought them attention and adoration years before.

To be sure, little people are so cute and cuddly. Unfortunately, babies, like puppies and kittens, grow up. And the bigger they get, the harder they are to conquer.

There's a story in the Old Testament (Numbers 13 and 14) of the 12 spies who went into the Promised Land to check it out before the Israelites moved in. That was a big mistake. It would have been better for them just to have marched right in and dealt with everything as it came. Instead, ten of the spies came back and said: "We felt like grasshoppers next to them, and that's what we looked like to them!" (Numbers 13:33 NLT) Defeat is automatically assured when you see yourself smaller and infinitely weaker than the opposing forces.

If the spies could have only remembered that babies grow up, and baby giants grow up to be really big – like bigger than their babies. If they could have remembered that, for every year they waited, there would be more baby giants. But somehow they forgot this practice of procreation and persuaded the people not to go in spite of how beautiful it was.

My point is this: Baby behavior, unchecked, will get bigger and bigger as the child gets bigger. Little problems, unresolved now, will grow to be giant problems later. Unfortunately, too many of us have let bad behavior go so long that we look at our teenager and despair that we are ever going to resolve the issues.

Mark Twain once wrote about the raising of children by saying that once a child turns 12, you should put them in a cider barrel with the cork left off. Then, when they turn 15, you must cork the barrel and not let them out until they are 25.

That approach would be highly discouraged, even in his day, but the key is that you cannot conquer by outright war. Instead, you have to use the same strategies your children used to overcome and conquer you. It takes prayer, planning, strategizing, and most of all, a will to win. You have to outsmart them just as they have outwitted you. You must find their buttons. The most important thing to understand is that conventional methods won't work in today's society. Conventional methods like: "You do it because I told you to." "Don't backtalk me. I'm your mother." How about this one? "You're grounded for good." Now that one really "scares" them. Your kids know once you have had a good night's rest, the grounding *for good* really meant, "Until I wake up tomorrow morning."

One of the most successful strategies children use today is the *divide and conquer* method. If they can get mom and dad to argue over their behavior or request, they know they are going to win.

In the following pages you will find strategies that have proven to be very successful in dealing with my own children and hundreds of other parents' little people. This is not intended to be an exhaustive book on discipline, nor is it intended to be a clinical treatise. Rather, the purpose of this book is to give hope to the despairing parent who is ready to give up, raise the surrender flag, and become the servant to the *Royal Pain* to whom they gave birth. For that matter, this includes anyone you adopt or to whom you provide care for any period of time.

Just one final word of caution: Do not show this battle plan to the invaders. Part of the secret to taking back your territory is to come upon them when they least expect it.

IF PARENTING IS A THREE RING CIRCUS, HOW COME I'M NOT THE RINGMASTER?

CHAPTER ONE
The best ringmasters are cheerleaders

We don't accomplish anything in this
world alone...and whatever happens
is the result of the whole tapestry of
one's life and all the weavings of
individual threads from one to
another that creates something.
— SANDRA DAY O'CONNOR

I love the smell of canvas, the suspense and excitement of watching *near misses*, and watching people doing stunts I would never think of doing. And, I love cotton candy. In short, I love the circus. It's a bit confusing to watch, but I love the three-ring circuses. Something is going on all the time.

I'll admit, it's hard to watch all three rings at the same time: The flying trapeze in one, the elephants in another and trick dogs in the next, plus horses galloping around all three. Wow, what a sight! How could everything be happening all at once? How could one acrobat fly through the air and catch the hands of another who is swinging by his legs and arrive at the right point at the right time? How could another stand on the backs of two horses racing around the arena so effortlessly without them forcing the rider to stretch beyond her limits? And what about the coordination of the elephants, the dogs, the lions and tigers, the sword swallower, the jugglers, clowns, and all the other acts?

Practice. That's it. Lots and lots of practice. Just as important as practice is to the success of the performance, you must have the full cooperation of your partner – be it human or animal. If you don't have the full support of the other, you might as well not be in the show.

Aside from the relentless practice required to make the act smooth and successful, you need a Ringmaster. You know, the guy that introduces you, the one who coordinates the whole show. More importantly, he's the one who gets everyone excited about seeing you. If you goof, he's the one who gets the audience to rally behind you to try it again. When you do something phenomenal, he's the one who gets everyone to cheer. When your act is all over, he rallies the people to believe in you, applaud for you, and makes your exit as smooth as possible. In short, the Ringmaster makes your appearance in public as graceful as possible.

Circuses work because everyone works together under the watchful eye of the Ringmaster. It takes a dedication to what you are doing. It takes focus, encouragement, and consistency. Can you begin to imagine someone on the flying trapeze deciding to change the act in the middle? That's when someone gets hurt.

So, if parenting is a three-ring circus and you are the Ringmaster, there are three ground rules you must establish right from the beginning. These are non-negotiable issues.

COOPERATION

Marriage takes a whole lot of cooperation to work successfully. It takes behind the scenes planning and strategizing – much more so when you have children. When you and your spouse come through the "curtain" of your private bedroom, your children need to know you are united in your position, with the commitment that no issues are to be resolved in front of them. The point of encounter with the children should be a rallying point – preparing them for their "public presentations."

Being the curious type all my life I had wondered where all those acts came from. As a teenager I got my chance. I sneaked around behind the Big Top and watched the array of acts getting ready to go on stage. I saw some arguing with each other. It didn't look so great back there; so I rushed back in just in time to see the same couple who were arguing moments before, put on a flawless performance in front of the audience.

Arguments should never be in the presence of the children. They, as a rule, don't know the reasons for the arguments between Mom and Dad unless, of course, they deliberately intend to create divisiveness between the parents. Most generally, all they know is there is an argument, and it just might be over them.

Every child, at some stage in their life, wants to mend the relationship between arguing parents, solve the problem and assure the adults that everything is *all right*. When divorce happens they will often blame themselves for not being able to *fix the problem.*

During the times you are tempted to argue in front of your children you must ask yourself, "Is my position more important than demonstrating a cooperative front to the children?" Generally not, unless it is related to abuse of some sort. That's not the time to argue, but rather the time to take decisive action to protect the child. This brings me to my second non-negotiable point.

PROTECTION AND SAFETY

Besides making parenting a cooperative effort, it's important that you do not demean or abuse a child. Can you ever picture a Ringmaster blaming or demeaning an act or actor in front of an audience? Absolutely not. That's when the Ringmaster rallies behind the mistakes and enthusiastically encourages the audience to cheer the actor on and provide the support and faith to try it again.

As adults, my siblings and I have talked about the fact that, in spite of how much we loved our mother, she never appeared to take any action to prevent the abuse our father handed out. It was almost as if she were powerless to help. If she ever felt bad about it, we did not know. As we entered adulthood we were certainly not interested in casting more heartache on her by mentioning it.

Some parents believe in absolute *ownership* of their children and don't see the necessity of giving them encouragement. They feel the only way to keep a child from going astray is to correct, scold, and punish. The problem is: Many of those *owned* children don't survive their childhood because they don't have a will to survive. Many suffer from adolescent depression. Of those who do, some resort to crime or accept less in life than what God intended for them to be.

According to my siblings my father seemed to have a passion to correct all my mistakes with violent responses that were in excess of how he treated them. Words such as *dummy, stupid, idiot, sissy,* and a few other choice words were a constant part of his vocabulary. What seemed most important to him was that his *sissy* son grow up with the *correct* vocabulary.

One of the severest beatings I had was over a simple announcement to him that Gertrude's water cup was *overflowing.* You see, we lived on a dairy farm, and my chore was to clean the water cups, the mangers, and feed the cows.

As soon as I made this announcement to my father, he hit me with a side blow to the face with his fist. This knocked me into the trench, covering me with manure from head to foot. He pulled me out of the trench and whaled on me and kicked me until he ran out of breath. His last words to me in that assault were, "No son of mine is going to talk like a city slicker. That water cup is not *overflowing*, it's running over." I was 14 at the time.

Do you want to know what I was the most sensitive about as an adult? Correctness. Not that *running over* is better than *overflowing*, but I had such fear of not saying the right words to satisfy my father it carried over into adulthood. For example, I found myself correcting someone telling a familiar story if they didn't get it right. Then, I took a speech class and stumbled over a story because I wanted to be accurate. The professor stopped me and said, "It is not as important to have all the facts correct as it is for your audience to feel like a part of the story. Now, start over and forget issues such as times, dates, locations, and names. Make me want to listen."

I never had a desire to call my children or my wife *dummy, idiot, stupid*, or any other demeaning name. I had been subjected to that so long I felt the hurt, as an adult, when I heard those words. For years, however, I had to bite my tongue to keep from correcting my family when they would tell a story that wasn't the same as I understood it to be. I continually had to say to myself, "This is their story, not mine. It is not important that they get the details correct. They are telling it from their heart and experience. How dare I intrude?" It then became my responsibility to be as enthusiastic about their story as the other listeners.

This type of carry over from childhood is well known in the counseling world. Allow me to share one more story to demonstrate the validity of this reality.

It wasn't that Franklin's parents were poor. On the contrary, both parents worked outside the home and had good jobs. The problem was that Franklin's parents spent more than they made. So, money was in short supply for some of the basic necessities.

Franklin remembers going to junior high and high school with holes in his shoes. When I say shoes, I mean just one pair. That's it. Rain, shine, church, sports – it was always the same pair of shoes.

At age 13 Franklin was becoming increasingly self-conscious about his appearance and desire to *fit in*. It was then that Franklin remembers his mom coming home with a new coat. He was happy that his mom had gotten the coat, but also a tad bit jealous. Out of curiosity, he asked his mom how much the coat cost.

Franklin was 50 when he related to me that he couldn't remember how much the coat had cost. He remembered only that he whistled and said, "I could have had two new pair of shoes for that price." He hadn't meant anything malicious. After all, he was only 13. Within minutes his father, who was outside, heard about the comment. He called Franklin outdoors, out of sight of everyone else, and started beating on him, almost to the point of unconsciousness.

The aftermath of that beating was that for years Franklin could not bring himself to owning more than two pair of shoes. He got married with his socks exposed as he knelt at the altar. He graduated from college with a different pair of shoes, but those too had been worn so much there were holes in them.

When his wife would attempt to buy him shoes he would protest that the two pair he had were plenty. Subconsciously, Franklin was living out the fear instilled in him during his early teens. It was still difficult at his present age, but he was beginning to enjoy wearing shoes with good heels and solid soles – thanks to his wife's persistence.

The bottom line to the fears, inhibitions, and joys of adulthood has its basis in the experiences of childhood.

SUPPORT AND AFFIRMATION

This isn't really a hard task. You just have to get used to complimenting rather than reprimanding. You have to begin thinking about what positive responses you will get if you compliment and affirm rather than criticize. The tone and volume of your voice, along with your body language, tell much more about your intent than the actual words. Body language also includes *looks*. Have you ever had someone give you a dirty look? Your pet can even tell what is a dirty look over a *so-glad-to-see-you* look.

Have you ever watched a parent humming, rolling their eyes, tapping a pen on the desk, or anything that would tell a child that they weren't going to listen to them anymore? It is guaranteed that when they get old enough to avoid retribution, they will develop their own obnoxious behavior to let the parent know they don't want to listen to them anymore.

Being supportive also means as you develop a creative method of disciplining, you make certain it is safe. Being dangerous with your children will instill far more fear in them than love.

Affirming a child has a valuable component in public. That means you do not embarrass your children in front of peers or adults. No amount of creativity is worth demeaning or embarrassing a child.

Children are not meant to be playthings – tossing them in the air or throwing them back and forth between individuals. The same is true with shaking a child. There are a lot of health risks and potential injuries that can happen to a child in those situations. The same is true by holding them down against their will. If they say they can't breathe, believe them and promptly give them relief. Just because they can talk does not mean they are not losing their breath.

Extensive tickling of a child can lead a child to some involuntary actions such as wetting their pants or cause them to be angry.

The following chapters are intended to help you be the best Ringmaster you can be as you spur your children on to greatness.

REVIEW

- Good parenting takes cooperative support from both parents.

- Demeaning behavior or words to or about a child are counterproductive, wrong and abusive.

- Do not bring into your parenting agendas anything from your own childhood that is demeaning or unhealthy.

- Obnoxious habits you developed to control your child will come back to spite you as your children grow into adulthood.

- Make certain all discipline is safe.

- Do not embarrass a child. He will find it difficult to forget or forgive.

IF PARENTING IS A THREE RING CIRCUS, HOW COME I'M NOT THE RINGMASTER?

CHAPTER TWO

Fear under the big top

Civilization is the process of
setting man free from men.
— AYN RAND

Let us not be content to wait and
see what will happen, but give us
the determination to make the
right things happen.
— PETER MARSHALL

I felt a chill crawl down my spine as I listened to a caseworker describe the circumstances of a 12 year old who had been chained to a post in his parents' barn for stealing food. Maybe it was the instant memory of being chained to a tree when I was two that sent the shivers along my spine.

A couple things the caseworker told me made this story even sadder. Trying to be as positive as possible, he said the boy weighed at least 37 pounds. He must be just a bunch of bones covered with skin, I thought to myself. What was more disturbing was the caseworker's comment about this boy's faith. "I don't know if he'll ever be able to trust and love God, or anyone else, for that matter."

Haunted for many years by my own fears of a god who was hateful and vengeful, I had a passion to help show him that the real God loves us, nurtures us, and revives our souls again. I had this urgency to share with him the scope of love that transcends bitterness and hatred so that, one day, he could be a caring adult rather than vengeful himself. However, I couldn't tell him. He had to experience it for himself. It would take time.

Six years after our first introduction, the skinny child was a young man graduating from high school. I asked him how he felt about God now that he had been in a safe and nurturing adoptive home for so long.

"For years," he explained. "I would wake up from nightmares of getting whipped and chained inside the barn because I tried to sneak some food after my parents went to bed. I was so hungry I thought I was going to die. I was afraid that God was like that too and was really scared, but not anymore. I didn't realize anyone could love me as much as God does."

"Are you bitter," I queried?

"I could be, but what's the use? I wouldn't need mean parents to destroy me, I would do it to myself."

As one looks back upon the history of the world you discover a consortium of examples of discipline with two basic themes – anger and punishment. As a matter of fact, it is so ingrained upon our lives that it seems to be rather natural.

The idea that so many glean from the Old Testament is that God is to be feared because He is a mean and punitive God. Much of that mentality, however, has come from the pagan history that crept into the worship of the true God. For example, in ancient Babylonian history their god Marduk made man out of the mangled corpses of his enemies. This meant that if man displeased him, he would destroy him and start over again.

The Israelites spent 300 years residing in Egypt, first as guests, and then as slaves. They could not help but have the theology and tradition of the fearful gods of Egypt rub off on them. This was exemplified when, standing on the shores of the Red Sea, they contended that God and Moses led them there to be slain (Genesis 14).

Even amidst the culture of the four millenniums that engulfed the Old Testament, where God is depicted similarly to those of the pagan gods, one can catch glimpses of a wonderful and loving God who would do anything to save us from the tyranny of the wicked world in which we live.

Beginning in Genesis where Adam and Eve sinned, there is not a fearsome God, as some would depict. Rather, here is depicted a loving God who knows where they are all the time. He only asks, "Where are you?" to get Adam and Eve to identify for themselves what has happened. Because God did not want to intrude upon their now sinful lives without first knocking, He asked that question. Adam, in turn, knowing God loved them, responded by saying, "I was afraid because I was naked." (Genesis 3:9,10 NLT)

The Old Testament is replete with stories of God's passionate love. The Book of Hosea, and Hosea's love for his prostituting wife, Gomer, was to be an example of how God could not give up on the prostituting Israelites. Then there's the Psalmist who never fails to find reason to praise the Lord for His loving mercy, forgiveness, and His watch care over His children. Hey, that's us!

So, contrary to the god Marduk, the real God made man because He loved humanity and wanted to share the beauties of love and the wonders of His creation. He even created man with the ability to procreate so mankind could understand the passion of love that He felt. He loved so much that He set up an escape plan – prior to creation – in case man was to sin.

God didn't seem to be able to get His love across any other way so He sent His Son to live and die – even forever, if necessary, so that we might live. It was not an emergency plan either – it was the escape plan created out of love before the *foundation of the world.*

Jesus came to demonstrate the love of God in practical terms: If someone is hungry – feed him. If someone is sick or imprisoned – visit him (Matthew 25). If someone is injured or mistreated – care for him, and if you can't personally, find someone who can (Luke 10:30-35). If someone spits on you – forgive him (Matthew 5:11). The list goes on.

One clear message Jesus portrayed in a world of indifference was that children had value and were to be treated as such. They were not to be considered of lesser value or a piece of property, to be treated at will or on a whim but, in fact, were and are the epitome of the Kingdom of Heaven.

There are several themes God wants us to understand that are in direct contrast to the themes of the world and to false gods.

God's rules don't change (James 1:17). There are consequences for our behavior (Romans 1). He is merciful and gracious and He will always love us (Romans 8:34-39). He wants to save us from the burden of our sins (Matthew 11:29). Because of that, He doesn't give up on us (Hebrews 13:5).

But wait! That's what this book is all about. How to deal with children and, in fact, other people the way Jesus would want you to.

These practical concepts and illustrations are to help those who have to struggle with their emotions when someone does something bad either deliberately or accidentally. It's all about "love, joy, peace, patience, kindness, goodness, faithfulness, gentleness and self control." (Galatians 5:22 NLT)

This book is about generational healing. It's about helping the next generation of adults and parents catch a glimpse of what healthy love and respect for their children can do to enhance enthusiasm for life and respect for each other. And this present generation of parents is the best place to begin.

REVIEW

- Anger is not a reliable or appropriate way to discipline. It only lends itself to provoking anger in the child.

- If you wish your children to love and respect you when they become adults – demonstrate love and respect for them as children.

- God's rules don't change and neither should ours.

- There are consequences for our behavior.

- Children have value and need to be treated as such.

CHAPTER THREE

Trouble in the training arena

Be kind, for everyone you meet is

fighting a battle.

— PLATO

It is foolish to wait for your ship to

come in unless you have sent one out.

— ALFRED A. MONTAPERT

Everyone in the early stages of their life messed their pants (rather, diapers). And I am certain that will continue to be the case in the future. Unless, of course, you grew or grow up in a culture where clothing was not used. In those cases... never mind.

The excitement of childhood should never be interrupted by the fear of reprisal if the child does something wrong. This is especially true with potty training. Of the three most exciting milestones of early childhood (walking, talking and potty training) parents seem to be the most focused on not having to deal with diapers any longer.

To be sure, parents gasp, cheer, applaud and give a child hugs and rewards when they first say "da da" or "ma ma" or take their first step from the chair to the coffee table. Why is it, however, we never seem to be pleased when our child learns to say no? Where did they learn the word? It isn't because it is not a complex or compound word. Rather, it's because they have heard that word more often than any other single word from their caregivers.

It's been said that by the time a child turns four he will have said "no" over 18,000 times. I have heard that quoted so many times but I don't know to whom to give credit. My point being, have you ever wondered how many times we say no to the same child in that same time span? It's not that the child just picks up the word "no" when it is being addressed directly to them, but there is an additional caveat: Consider how often we tell our spouses no, when we really mean to say, "give me more time to think about it." Or, "I won't accept that idea until it becomes mine." That stubborn word "no" jumps up in front of our faces more often than we realize.

The best strategy for the young ones is to use complete sentences rather than the single syllable word unless it is a matter of emergency.

Now that I have digressed a bit, let's get back to the potty training. Potty training seems to be a never-ending ordeal and just gradually disappears on its own. All parents are relieved when the event happens, but can never place a time, date or event when the transition happened for good. The reason? Many times a child can be so happy to have friends to play with or just concentrating on their own personal activity that they totally forget to take care of some basic bodily functions until it is too late. Then, when the *accident* does happen, they are embarrassed.

This frequently happens in winter when parents bundle their children up against the cold and snow. The child then is escorted to the door and sent out to play with the other children. Time passes too quickly when you are having fun. But, somewhere during the playtime, they have the urge to *go*. They know full well if they went to the house they wouldn't get their clothes off in time anyway, so they just do their business and keep on playing. This usually happens during that transition time between diapers and total control.

If a child knows they are going to be punished because of the *accident*, they will hold off as long as possible before any declaration of guilt. Or, they may try to take care of the situation themselves, thus making a further mess. Fear of reprisal is usually the greatest causative factor in prolonging the potty training.

Let me put it this way: Once a child has learned to walk and is fairly confident and they happen to trip and fall, do you run over to them and scold them, tell them they are a klutz and threaten them if they trip again? Absolutely not! You pick them up, nurse their wounds and give them as much encouragement as possible.

Potty training should be practiced in the same manner. But because it is socially unacceptable to smell bad, we want our child to be the youngest human ever known in history to be potty trained. Some parents have jokingly suggested that when a child is old enough to say the word "pooh" they ought to be changing their own diapers.

I will never forget the night I received a call from the emergency room of a hospital near where I lived. It was close to midnight. I had already been asleep for a couple of hours, so it took me a few moments to register that it was not my shoe that was ringing. The doctor explained to me that there was a child in the emergency room that needed immediate shelter care. The Department of Social Services had taken the child into protective custody, and I was elected to find a placement for him.

The sterile aroma of the emergency room was punctuated by the plaintiff cry of a young child. Interspersed with his cries was the word "Mamma." Before I even saw the child, the doctor ushered me into the room where x-rays of a small child were tacked up to the light boards. "I want you to notice the bones on this child's extremities," he said. Immediately I noticed a fracture on the child's left arm close to the wrist.

The doctor proceeded to point out numerous hairline fractures on both legs and arms, which had healed over time. This child was barely two years old and already had experienced eight broken bones. The parents brought him in this time only because obvious swelling had occurred and the child would not quit crying. The boy's mother's excuse was, "He messed his pants and I punished him to let him know that was not appropriate."

This boy's mother, by her anger and punishment, had automatically prolonged potty training.

Recently I was getting my hair cut by a lovely beautician who wasn't nosy about my affairs. She wanted to talk about her 10-month-old son who was just learning to walk. Curious as to her observations about raising small children, I asked, "what is your biggest challenge in raising your 10-month-old son?"

"I'm afraid for him because he has no fear," was her response. "He would go with anyone. He will walk through any open door. That's what scares me."

I wondered, at that moment, about how some children develop a sense of fear. Some parents endeavor to create a healthy fear in their children through education, proper disciplining, etc. Other children become fearful because of the abuse they experience from their own parents. Here's an example.

Everyone called him Sammy. He didn't like that. He wanted to be called Sam. After all, he was 13 years old and was *grown up*. There was only one problem Sam had, and that was bowel and bladder control problems. He wet his bed by night and messed his pants by day. He smelled bad. To make matters worse, all the other young people in our Youth Ranch (see Appendix) made fun of him and steered clear of him.

At the same time Sam was at our Ranch, there was a young man by the name of Antonio, who was 16. His size wasn't important. He was one of those young men who was a natural born leader, and frankly, no one even thought of messing with him without a fear of reprisal. You see, he was angry that he had to be there. It seems his mother brought him to us with him thinking it was a summer of fun, only to discover it was a controlled atmosphere. And when he got a whiff of Sam, he was even angrier yet.

One day a van load of the young people was driving off the Ranch to go hiking. In less than a mile, the taunting and teasing of Sam began. Within the time it took the van to go the next mile, a fight had broken out. It was Sam against six other young men. The driver pulled off the road just as Antonio took an uppercut from Sam. Sam threw open the door and began to run. Determined to get even, Antonio bolted from the van as well. The race was on!

Sam ran like a bear was after him. Actually, he was not far from wrong. Sam dove through a fence and was on his feet running before Antonio could figure out how to manipulate the fence without getting cut on the barbed wire. He lost a bit of time on that hurdle, but he was determined to catch Sam and give him the "beating of his life."

The rest of the boys and the driver stood along side the road and watched as Sam and Antonio went over the bank a half-mile away and disappeared. The only thing to do was to go back to the Ranch and get the rest of the staff to search for the two marathon runners.

Several hours passed, and no one found any trace of them. Were we to expect the worst? Did they get lost? Did Antonio hurt Sam? What was happening and

where? Our questions were answered just before sunset.
Antonio came walking back on campus with his arm
around Sam's shoulders.

They were both scratched, bruised, and wet from having
run through swamp land, underbrush, across the river twice
and finally collapsing on the bank of the river too exhausted
to fight. What transpired at that moment was a gift from
heaven for both the 13- and 16-year-old boys.

Sam, still sobbing, had poured out to Antonio that he
had been sexually and physically abused ever since he
could remember. He didn't really want to be the way he
was, but he just couldn't help it.

Children who have suffered from sexual abuse in early
childhood will often suffer from enuresis and encupresis to
subconsciously protect themselves from the predator.

As Antonio stood in front of a group of puzzled adults
and teens alike with his arm still around Sam, he
announced, "Sam doesn't smell anymore." (Whom was he
kidding? We could still smell him from a distance.) To
make certain he got his point across he repeated it again.
"Sam doesn't smell anymore." Then he explained what he
had learned on the bank of the river. Antonio continued,
"And if anyone ever teases Sam again, you will answer to
me personally."

What a gift to Sam! What a gift to Antonio! What a
gift to all of us – adults and teenagers alike! A miracle
began to happen in Sam's life. He now had a protector.
He now had someone who accepted him regardless of
how bad he smelled. Sam's accidents happened less and
less frequently up until the day he was to return home.
On that day Antonio was there beside Sam with a big hug

to assure him he was available if any one messed with him again.

Believing in a child furthers their growth much faster than disapproving of their behavior.

Review

- The excitement of childhood should not be interrupted by the fear of reprisal.

- Children should learn to fear dangers but never have to fear their parents.

- Children will subconsciously do things to protect themselves from known predators.

- Believing in a child furthers their growth much faster than disapproving of their behavior.

CHAPTER FOUR

Humor vs the unwilling

A cheerful heart is good medicine, but a broken spirit saps a person's strength.—

PROVERBS 17:22 NLT

Laughing is good exercise – it's like jogging on the inside.

— ANONYMOUS

Using humor to get your point across is not a new concept. God used it many times when no other option seemed to work. Two classic stories in the Old Testament illustrate this and had a profound affect on both of the men involved.

The first story I'd like to share is the story of Balaam, found in Numbers 22 through 24. The synopsis of the story is this: Balak, the king of the Moabites, saw the Israelites camped next to his kingdom on their way to the promised land. He had heard about what they had done to the Amorites and wanted to make certain that before he went to war with them, he had taken advantage of every opportunity to assure victory for himself. To whom should he go, but to a prophet of the same God as those of the Israelites? Smart thinking. All he needed to do was pay the prophet enough to make it worth his while.

When the ambassadors first came to Balaam and offered the bribe, he refused because God told him not to go. So Balak sent some high ranking officials with more money and a promise of a higher position. Apparently, Balaam wasn't real strong on his decision, because he invited them to stay overnight so he could think and pray about it. Balaam was acting a bit childish. He didn't take "no" from God the first time. I don't know what he was thinking. Maybe he thought he could wear God down.

I'm certain God figured Balaam would pout about it if he didn't go, so God said, "Okay, you can go." This is where God gets really creative. If Balaam wasn't going to listen to Him, maybe he'd listen to his donkey. Only twice in the Bible does a creature talk to a human. Once the Devil used a serpent to talk to Eve. And this time, God lets the donkey tell Balaam what she really thought of him. The amazing part of this story is that Balaam talked back to his donkey without a flicker of amazement. He was too angry to realize what a *donkey* he was himself!

The other classic story of God's creative humor was when He told Jonah to go to Nineveh to let the people know that He was going to destroy the city. All of a sudden Jonah realizes he has a non-refundable ticket to Spain and can't make the appointment. He makes a beeline to Joppa and gets on board a boat heading west – far west – like to Spain.

Here's the amazing part of God's humor. He could have sunk the boat in the harbor; He could have chased Jonah to Nineveh with a swarm of bees, or a number of other things. I can imagine when Jonah refused to go and headed towards the *cruise ship* that God bade him farewell and wished him a safe trip knowing full well how He was going to get his attention.

The Bible doesn't say how far out in the Mediterranean they had gone before the storm hit, but it was a bad one. Desperation set in among the crew, and they started throwing the cargo overboard. That is when they found Jonah – fast asleep in the hold of the ship.

Jonah finally confesses it is his fault that the storm hit with such fury; but he wasn't about to go to Nineveh, so he told them just to throw him overboard. He would rather die than see any one of the Ninevites saved, even if it meant not doing what God wanted.

This reminds me of my brother, Rick, when my three brothers and I were in our early teens. My mother was a soft touch, and we all knew it. If she decided to spank us, one would plead our case in front of her to distract her while the other three would run to the bedroom to pad their bottom ends. The first one out would switch with the one defending our case so we all could get padding on the critical spot.

We really didn't need to do that, because when Mom spanked us it was so soft that we found it necessary to cry to make her feel like she had accomplished her mission.

One day we were caught red-handed playing with the chainsaw. We thought we were far enough away from the house to muffle the noise. She came charging at us with a leather strap. Oh, oh, we were in serious trouble! We were too far away from the house to get any padding on. She started with Phil, the oldest. On cue he would cry. Sometimes he missed his cue and yelled before the stroke of the strap.

When she felt that she had accomplished her mission with Phil, she turned to the next in line – Rick. Rick wasn't about to be spanked, so he turned to walk away. He was heading towards the woods. Rick was the determined type. He would have walked as far as necessary to avoid the spanking – even if it was into the next county.

When Mom told Phil to go get him, Rick turned and stormed back towards Mom and yelled, "Go ahead, kill me! See if I care."

That was the same with Jonah. He didn't care how merciful and gracious God was; he would rather die than go to Nineveh.

After much persuasion, Jonah convinced the crew to throw him overboard. Death would come in moments – or so he thought. But God had other plans: three days and three nights in the luxury hotel of the sea. Primitive as it was with no electricity and all, he knew he was either doomed to die a slow, rotting death or face the God he had run from.

It took Jonah three days before he decided he wanted to pray for deliverance. It wasn't long before the fish vomits him up on the shore. His first question to God was, "What do you want me to do?" God's answer was the same. "Go to Nineveh and do what I told you to do in the first place."

I think Jonah had to ask for directions from the closest fisherman because he probably didn't have a clue where he was. Maybe there were three or four fishermen he had to ask before he found one who wouldn't pass out from the sight of him. (Seaweed around his neck, a pale ghostly complexion from the gastric juices of the fish, and this guy wanted to go east to Nineveh).

There are countless other stories both in the Old and New Testaments that verify that Divinity has a sense of humor. Therefore, it might be wise to use it on children, and even adults who are acting a bit rebellious.

You see, a person doesn't have a clue what you are thinking if you are smiling. But, if you scowl or express anger, they know full well what you're thinking.

Lisa redefined *bad hair day* at least three times a day. That is the reason she was at our youth ranch. She not only had several "bad hair days" every day, but she wanted to be in control.

One day Lisa didn't feel as if she was being heard, and she definitely wasn't getting what she wanted. In desperation she ran up to me and angrily demanded to be taken home. I asked her why she wanted to go home. Her response was a bit more graphic than I can share, but she declared that the rules stunk, the staff, the food and I, all stunk equally as bad. "I can't stand to stay here a minute longer," she yelled in desperation.

I smiled. You see, situations like these demand more than a defense of your position. It is not the time to try to defend your integrity, your lineage, your philosophy, and the dietary benefits of the food or even *order* her to get her act together. So smiling was the best option.

Her immediate reaction was, "What?"

"I can't let you go," I responded.

"Why not? You're the boss. You can let me out of here if you want."

"I can't," I said. "Because there are two young men who are so madly in love with you they want to marry you when you get to be an adult. But they don't want to marry you with your lousy, rotten, stinking, good-for-nothing attitude. So they paid us a lot of money with the hopes we could help you get the inside of you as beautiful as the outside of you." I paused a minute for the compliment and the reality of her behavior to sink in.

"Besides, we spent all the money and we don't have it to give back. So you are going to have to stay."

"You're lying to me," she blurted out.

"You're right, I am." I was careful not to lose the point of the discussion now. "If you don't stay here long enough so we can help you get the inside of you as beautiful as the outside, you are going to go through relationship after relationship. And one of them you just might want to keep, but you can't because you are too difficult to live with."

We talked for another ten minutes about the value of becoming a positive person. She finally agreed to stay and started to walk away. After taking a few steps, she stopped and turned back towards me. "Are there really two?" she asked. I assured her there were going to be lots of young men who would be pursuing her. That was why it was so important to stabilize her attitude and emotions.

The use of hyperbole and contrast is an important component in the art of using humor with people of all ages. This is especially true for the teens that have not yet lost their spirit of wonderment and fully understand that exaggeration is an effective tool. After all, have you ever seen a teenager who hasn't practiced this art? They might go into shock by your using their tried and true methods on them.

Jesus used this method in a very effective manner. He once said. "It is easier for a camel to go through the eye of a needle than for a rich man to enter the kingdom of heaven." (Matthew 19:24 NLT) He compared the faith of a mustard seed to being large enough to move a mountain.

When you use hyperbole on your children – make certain that they clearly understand that you are serious about the message regardless of the absurdity of the statement. You are merely using excessive exaggeration to contrast it with their own behavior.

Lest you think that this idea has no merit in practicality, let me share an incident within my own family where this principle was used effectively.

One of my son's many methods to manipulate me was the use of compliments. I had pretty well mastered the art of avoiding most of his other subtle and not so subtle ways of getting what he wanted. But compliments from a 16-year-old son are rare, so I relished those tokens of appreciation for my intelligence, aptitude and mechanical abilities. (He grew up watching me restore antique automobiles for a hobby.)

One day as Craig and I were driving along in silence, he said, "Dad, you were so good at rebuilding and restoring those old cars, and you have completely given that up. Wow! What a waste of talent. Dad, could you show me how to do that before you completely lose all the knowledge that it has taken you years to develop?"

I was about to open my mouth to tell him he had to have an antique to work on in order for me to show him how. We didn't have one, and I wasn't going to buy one. I was going to lecture him about how expensive it was and about the low to non-existent financial return. I had done it because of an appreciation of old cars, and I had lost my desire to appreciate them that much anymore.

I didn't get one word out of my mouth before he continued, "Of course, we are going to need something to restore. But, Dad, I'd settle on something simple just so you could teach me what you know. If you could just show me the art once, then I would be good to go on my own. You wouldn't have to spend any time yourself. You could just serve as my consultant."

That did it! I had been suckered and suckered good. My son wanted to learn from me – his father. I turned off the freeway, and we started to *cruise the drag* for a 1950's vintage auto so that he would not be discouraged trying to find parts.

It was our *bonding time*, and I had been complimented into total submission.

Before we made it home that evening we had found the *perfect* car. It fit all my expectations. It was from the '50's, parts were still available, and it looked like an easy ground-up restoration. The body was pretty straight, it ran, and it stopped. After haggling a bit on the price, we came to an agreement. "Great," I said to the salesman, "We'll take it!"

We put our deposit down and went home to announce our proud *togetherness acquisition*. When Craig explained excitedly to his mother why we were late and what we had just bought, she gave me the *look*. You know, that look that tells you a mistake has just been made, and it wasn't her that made it. Yes, that look.

Both Craig and I invested the rest of the evening persuading her that this was a good thing for a father and son to do together. "Just look at it this way, sweetheart." (To be sure, I was heavy on the *sweetheart*.) "It's like paying tuition for a class in auto restoration. Could you at least drop us off at the car lot tomorrow so we can drive it home?"

"Okay," she said. "But I don't want this project to take up the whole garage so I can't put my car in." We both gave her our assurance. Little did I realize my promise was going to be very short lived.

The next day dawned with the same excitement as a Christmas morning. Bonnie dropped us off, and Craig and I finished the final details of the purchase and were off with our newly acquired restoration project – a 1955 C-J 5 Jeep.

I was glad that it was less than ten miles to our house. The Jeep had so many air holes it would sink in a rain shower. Holes on top, many holes and cracks on the sides, and enough on the floor to let the fumes from a leaking exhaust pipe dance around our heads causing us to expand every available opening along the sides. The first thought was to roll down the window, which promptly shattered as it dropped unceremoniously to the bottom of the door.

Once we got home I bid my son farewell and told him I would be home early so I could help with a few principles of getting started – like labeling everything you take off to assure it can be put back in the right place.

Hurrying home that evening, I was greeted with Bonnie's car in the drive, but not in the garage. Oh, oh. This was a sure sign of pending doom. But, on the other hand, maybe the garage door opener wasn't working. Maybe I am looking at this too pessimistically, I thought. Just a slight mechanical failure, which I am sure I can fix.

I pushed the opener for my side of the garage. It was like a curtain rising on a play that had already begun. I was greeted with a totally stripped vehicle. I mean, the only things left together were the springs and steering wheel – both attached to the frame. I soon realized those were still attached only because of a lack of time.

As I ventured a look inside, I discovered the entire vehicle scattered across the expanse of a two-and-a-half-car garage. I thought for a moment of leaving town for a week. But a hasty retreat was squelched when Craig declared, "It's all right, Dad. Mom said I could use her side too for a couple of weeks."

Two weeks went by and then three, four, six and eight. Craig had cleaned and painted the frame. It actually looked impressive. But the fact remained that the car was still scattered throughout the garage. What made matters worse was that Craig was leaving for school in a couple weeks, and Bonnie wanted her side of the garage back.

One Friday morning I announced to Craig that we were going to clean the garage on Sunday and put the car back together so it looked like it was in one piece. "I am not about to restore this for you," I declared with some confidence. "Even if you have to drag this off with you on your honeymoon – should you ever think of marriage." He assured me he would be around on Sunday.

I got up bright and early and went to the garage to survey the damage and assess the possibility of putting this assortment of nuts, bolts, and metal parts back together as rapidly as it came apart. Craig's room was above the garage so I could tell that my imitation of reveille had been a success as I passed his room.

I heard the radio. I felt the aftershock of him plopping back onto his bed. Fifteen minutes went by and no further sign of movement. To be angry would give him an excuse not to help. I had to think of a plan to get his attention without storming up to his room in anger.

My eyes landed on the breaker box over in the corner of the garage. It would take some effort to make it there, but my determination was building as I dodged potentially hazardous objects in my quest for a special breaker.

I scanned the panel looking for the breaker switch to his room. Ah, victory, I thought as I flipped it to the off position. Now, I had to get away from there quick. I heard his feet hit the floor within seconds of the power outage. I heard him charge down the two flights of stairs. The door between the house and the garage swung open.

"Why did you turn my power off? You ruined my computer program," he declared in disgust.

I looked up at him. I was impressed as to how much taller the steps made his already six-foot-five-inch frame look. "Careful," I cautioned myself. "This giant needs someone else to blame."

"I didn't do anything," I declared innocently.

"My power is out, and my room is the only one affected."

"It wasn't me, honest. It was your landlord. And he says you are past due on your rent. He isn't going to turn it on until you pay up."

I could see the epiphany cross his mind. "Okay," he said meekly, "Could I have the power back on so I can get dressed?"

"I think that could be arranged."

Trusting that power was imminent, he disappeared. Five minutes went by and no Craig. Then I heard the shower. I'll give in to the fact he needs to be clean. But this shower went on so long I was almost convinced he was siphoning hot water from the next-door neighbors. To be sure, I turned off the valve to our hot water tank.

There was this blood-curdling scream. No, it was our hot water he was still using. Shucks! His scream was followed by loud footsteps down two flights of stairs, and a door being thrust open with incredible speed. "What did you do to the hot water?" he demanded.

"Nothing," I again declared innocently. I ventured a look. The bath towel wrapped around his tall frame barely appeared to do its job. His hair was coated with shampoo. "It must have been your electric company. Your electric bill is so far past due they are demanding immediate payment."

"Okay, Okay. Can you give me enough hot water to rinse the soap out of my hair and I promise I will be right down."

"I can't, but I am sure the power company will."

"Whatever," he said with a bit of resignation as he closed the door.

The rest of the day was wonderful. The car was back together and pushed out of the garage and under tarp in one day's time. I wasn't sure if it would ever run again, but all the pieces were in it, on it or hanging somewhere on its painted frame.

Humor is critical, hyperbole is essential, and the next chapter will let you in on another important ingredient to **success without distress**.

REVIEW

- Humor without sarcasm works wonders when nothing else will.

- A smile will do two things in a tense situation: 1. It will disarm or reduce tension, and will catch the verbal assailant off guard. 2. It will buy you time to think rather than react.

- Hyperboles are an effective tool in dealing with teens. As a matter of fact, it is so effective that your teens have been using it, or soon will be using it on you.

- Lectures are always ineffective.

IF PARENTING IS A THREE RING CIRCUS, HOW COME I'M NOT THE RINGMASTER?

CHAPTER FIVE
Creativity in the center ring

Start by doing what is necessary,

then do what is possible.

Suddenly you are doing

the impossible.

— ST. FRANCIS OF ASSISI

So few have imagination that

there are ten thousand fiddlers to

one composer.

— CHARLES G. KETTERING

I am convinced that children lay awake at night trying to figure out how to outsmart their parents. The problem is, they don't have to stay up very long in order to figure us out. That behooves us as parents to lay awake at night praying and figuring out how to outsmart them. Once you develop a creative posture in disciplining, life becomes much simpler.

I will never forget the story of a mother in Canada who was having a problem with her five-year-old son. The problem developed around shopping trips. Not having a baby sitter, she always took the young man along on those trips. Invariably, when they would go to the grocery store, he would walk or ride along and throw things in the cart, or out of it, depending on his likes and dislikes. As much as Mom tried to throttle the outbursts of "yuk," "no way," and "Mommy, I need this, get me this," she was perplexed about how to stop the destruction of the grocery store.

Not wanting to behave like some of the other mothers she saw slapping their children and threatening them with never seeing the inside of the store again, she contacted a friend who encouraged her to be creative.

Within two weeks she had it figured out and tried her creative experiment with wonderful success. She bought her destructive shopping companion a pair of pants that were two sizes too big for him. She then added to that component a pair of cute little suspenders. The young man thought he was in heaven because he now had baggy pants like the big boys.

In his little mind, I am sure he thought he had won the game. But Mom was not to be outsmarted by a five-year-old. The next time they went shopping, the little scamper got to wear his baggy pants with suspenders. As he walked proudly into the grocery store anticipating another wave of violence on some of the food products, mother abruptly brought him to a halt. With the speed of a gazelle, Mom had those suspenders off and in her purse. She then began pushing the cart as if nothing different had happened other than a pleasant exchange with her beloved son.

For the next hour, while mother was shopping, the little tyke was trailing behind Mom holding up his pants begging for his suspenders. It only took two trips to the store in that condition before he understood that he wasn't ever to pull things out of the cart or throw anything in the cart.

The older the child gets, the more creative you have to become. One of the keys is to discover his or her greatest weakness. I call it searching for the child's Achilles heel.

According to Homer in the Iliad – Achilles' mother, Thetis, wanting to immortalize him, held the young child by the heel and dipped him in the river Styx. Everything the *sacred waters* touched became invulnerable, but the heel remained dry and therefore unprotected.

When Achilles was still a boy, a *seer* prophesied that the city of Troy could not be taken without his help. Thetis was convinced that if her son went to Troy he would die. In a desperate move, she sent him to the court of Lycomedes' daughter, Deidameia. He was disguised as a maiden and for years escaped the watchful eyes of those searching for him. Odysseus, in a stroke of genius, placed swords, spears and armor among a display of women's clothing. Achilles was the only "maiden" to express fascination over the arsenal of weaponry. He was caught because he could not conceal his weakness and fascination for weapons of war.

Voila! What a wonderful thought. Checking out what your child is passionate about might also be your secret to discovering how you can get him or her to do what you wish with the least bit of resistance and conflict. The same is true with us as adults. Our greatest strengths can also be our greatest weakness. Here's a case in point:

Joan, a mother of five, came to see me out of desperation. It seemed that her 15-year-old son was ruling the house. What was worse, he was rallying the rest of the children to his side.

According to Joan, every day when Billy would come home from school, he raided the refrigerator. When she would tell him that an item was purchased for dinner or a meal later on, he would just laugh. He would act as the official taster in the court of jesters and then hand some of his spoils to the younger children, who would laugh with glee.

It was clear that Joan had lost control of her own house. What bothered her the most was she could not plan a meal if Billy showed up before it was on the table.

And, of course, he always did show – right after school.

Oh, I should tell you that Billy was no small child to be reckoned with. At 15, he was six foot four inches tall and weighed every bit of 240 pounds.

It was obvious that Billy's weakness was food but, "Was there anything else more important to Billy than food?" I asked Joan.

"Oh yes," she responded. "He lives for money. He saves every penny he can get because he wants to buy the nicest pickup he can get when he turns 16."

"What's his passion?" I queried. "Is money more important than food?" "That's why he raids the refrigerator when he gets home. He won't spend a dime at school. Even though I pack him a good lunch, he always seems to head for the refrigerator when he gets home."

One other piece of information I needed to know. Since he was a minor, who was the co-signer on his savings account? Mom confessed she was.

Strategically speaking, I suggested to Mom that she put a list of foods on the refrigerator that he could eat free of charge once he got home. Second, she was to list all the foods that he could not touch unless he was willing to pay for them. The price also needed to be listed beside the items in the event he wanted them anyway.

At the bottom of the list there would be a surcharge for those items for which Mom would have to make a special trip to the store due to the immediacy of her meal preparation. The surcharge was to be stiff – with mileage and time added.

Once a week, Mom would then tally up all the charges and withdraw that amount from her son's savings account.

A month later Joan was back in my office all smiles. It had worked like a clock. Billy was no longer taking things he wasn't supposed to because it was now clear to him what was okay to eat and what was not. Rarely did he have a snack attack that involved an item on the *for sale* list because money for a pickup had gone south in a hurry during the first two weeks.

The real key for Joan and her family was that she finally set some parameters and stuck to them by discovering what was important to her children and, hence, what was their Achilles heel.

Perhaps the most difficult time to be creative is when you are tired and when the children are extra fussy. You don't generally plan on being confronted with obstinate behavior when you have had an exceptionally rough day. However, if you do, shame on you. You are already gearing up for failure. Unfortunately, the surprises in life are the ones for which you are least prepared. That is the time to run to the bathroom, lock the door, and sit there until you have a plan in place.

Here is one of the things I discovered early on in the life of being a husband and a father. For every minute you fuss and insist on being left alone, and for every minute you scold or discipline the children for not behaving while you rest, you will spend at least 15 minutes recovering from the stress or making amends to them. Hence, 30 minutes of stubborn resistance or punishing your children for *disturbing the peace* will cause you 12 hours of remorse.

This is not a scientific study in the least, and maybe it is a little bit of a stretch. However, the fact remains that most adults have to spend much more time repairing the damage than it took causing it.

Many times a parent will punish a child because of behavior that is induced merely because they want attention. Then when you give them negative attention consistently they will learn to thrive on that. Hence, you perpetuate the very thing you dislike – negative behavior. The suggestion to run to the bathroom and lock the door is to encourage you to pick a strategy that is going to provide the attention your child needs and help you relax as well.

Our daughter, Kelly, was two years old when she contracted chicken pox. The nights seemed to be particularly rough because Bonnie and I wanted and needed our sleep. Kelly, I am sure, wanted her sleep as well. Realizing no one was going to get any sleep that night under the circumstances, and knowing Kelly liked to travel with me, I made a deal with Bonnie. I would take Kelly out for a drive so she could sleep if I could catch some rest in the morning. I'm not one who can just pace the floor or exercise on a treadmill. I have to be going somewhere. Further, I like to be productive. Aha! A moment of brilliance flashed before me.

I took Kelly's diapers to the laundromat to launder them there. While they were washing I drove around town. It was two o'clock in the morning so there wasn't much to do. Then again, this would be an ideal time to look at used cars because there would be no salesmen to intrude upon my meanderings.

True to form, Kelly went to sleep as we drove around. She even slept through my exits from our car to look at the rows of used cars. My activities did not go unnoticed however. After perusing a couple car lots, I saw red and blue lights of a police car in my rear view mirror.

Concerned about my excursion to the car lots that late at night, the officers wished to see my trunk to ascertain if there was a quantity of hubcaps or other specialty items there. After extensive investigation and interrogation, they accepted my confession of innocence and let me go to retrieve Kelly's diapers.

Needless to say, my little excursion to the laundromat took much longer than I had expected, courtesy of the local police department. To my amazement, that encounter made the early morning hours go by much quicker. By morning Bonnie was happy, Kelly had slept and I fell in a heap into bed. The satisfaction of not offending either brought sweet repose.

The key to being creative in these circumstances is to find something to do for your child that is going to inspire them, reduce their tension and offer respite for you as well. A couple examples to start your creative juices going might be offering to go to a fast food restaurant for supper or telling your children, "Today we are going to hunt for our own food." Then you pack a couple sandwiches for an emergency, take your children down to the river, pond, or anything that looks like water and let them fish. Then, you find a spot, a safe distance away, and watch.

If you psych yourself up to being upset you will be sure to expend much more energy than you would by doing something you all will enjoy, which guarantees strong family unity.

REVIEW

- Children generally lay awake at night figuring out how to outsmart their parents. Parents should do the same on behalf of their children. The problem is – children don't have to stay awake very long compared to the parents.

- Creativity is essential in discipline if one wishes to go beyond the lazy practice of getting angry and yelling and, perhaps, spanking.

- Do not presuppose you can manage your child just because you are older, wiser, bigger, and their parent.

CHAPTER SIX
Discipline vs punishment

*I would not waste my life in
friction when it could be turned
into momentum.*
— FRANCES WILLARD

*Give generously, for your gifts
will return to you later.*
— ECCLESIASTES 11:1 NLT

I have a couple of my own working definitions of punishment which are as follows:

Punishment is the emotional response to another's behavior that has less to do with their actions and more to do with the release of your emotional energy.

Punishment has little to do with one's misbehavior and a lot to do with the desire of another to inflict emotional or physical pain on the subject.

Discipline, on the other hand, deals with the consequences of one's own behavior. At that moment in time there is the opportunity to teach valuable lessons. Briefly speaking, this is your *teachable moment.* Hence the word "discipline." Those are golden opportunities to disciple one who has learned a valuable lesson without demeaning, ridiculing, or treating one in a condescending manner. Let me explain the difference.

If you are driving down the highway ten miles over the speed limit, and if you are the only one driving that speed, and you get a ticket – you just suffered the consequences of your own deliberate actions.

However, if you are driving down the highway ten miles over the speed limit, and everyone else is driving that fast or faster, and you get pulled over and get a speeding ticket – that's punitive.

Punishment or punitive responses are never fair, and they can leave feelings of resentment for years to come.

My wife and I lived in Montana for six years; the last year was in Polson, a beautiful little town on the south end of Flathead Lake. One day I had the occasion to be in St. Ignatius, one of those communities where blinking your eyes can cause you to miss half the town.

After completing my business, I cautiously drove out of town knowing full well that many small towns relish the revenue from speeding tickets. Feeling that I had gone way past the city limits, I began picking up speed. Almost instantaneously I noticed flashing red lights in my rearview mirror. I pulled over thinking the patrol car wanted to go by. Not so. He pulled in behind me and strolled up to my door with a grin that told me something ominous was about to happen to me.

"You were going 65 in a 35 mile-per-hour-speed zone," he commented as if he had recited that speech many times before.

I was incredulous. "How could that be?" I asked. "I am way out in the country."

"You see that sign up there?" he asked, pointing about a quarter of a mile further ahead. "That says, 'Leaving St. Ignatius City Limits.' I am going to have to give you a ticket. May I see your driver's license?"

I knew I had no defense. So I began searching for my driver's license. I looked in the pockets of my jacket which was lying in the passenger's seat. I searched the pockets of my trousers, my shirt, and in the glove box with no success.

I finally confessed to the officer that while I was sure I brought my billfold with me, I could not find it. Where-upon he politely said, "I'll let you go this time, but next time remember it is 35 clear past that sign." I thanked him profusely for being so kind.

Almost as an afterthought as he turned to go, he asked one more question that was to turn the tide of emotions. "By the way, what do you do for a living?"

"I'm a minister," I responded.

I no sooner got the word "minister" out of my mouth than he threw his hat to the ground and began cursing. Amidst the volley of profanity he assured me that I was not leaving that very spot until he had given me the biggest ticket I had ever seen.

Curious as to why my moment of grace had passed without my escaping, I ventured to ask him why he had changed his mind? Through his sputtering and fuming this is what he told me.

He said that before coming to St. Ignatius he was a deputy sheriff out of Missoula, Montana. Every Sunday morning a Catholic priest left his parish in Missoula and headed towards his parish in Hamilton, southwest of Missoula. He described how this priest in a black Cadillac would speed through town and out into the country. With his Chevrolet patrol car all warmed up, car in gear, foot on brake and hand on the switch for the red lights, he waited like a hawk for that priest to sail by his parked cruiser.

Every Sunday the priest ignored the red lights and siren. This cat and mouse exchange continued for almost a year before the patrolman standing by my window asked for a transfer.

"I vowed that the next priest or minister I stopped was going to pay for all the times that priest embarrassed me in the chase."

"And I suppose I am the 'very next minister' you have stopped?" I ventured to ask.

"You're darn tootin' you are."

As kind as I could I asked him why he never called for backup? He explained that he was a Catholic and did not want to incur any "extra penance" at confession. He wasn't even sure what he would do if the priest had ever pulled over. One thing he did know was it angered him.

Have you ever come home from work frustrated or angry at your boss or another employee, or even had a bad commute? Often those pent up emotions are taken inside your home, and you take your frustrations out on the children, who are just being children.

Without sounding too technical, what you are doing is called the "transference of emotions." Perhaps you stuffed your emotions all day long and now, in the security of your own home, you take your anxiety out on the ones you love. You have heard that writing letters to those you have issues with is healthy. Indeed it is. The key is to keep from sending them. I still have a couple such letters from years ago. Once in a while I come across them when we move. I am so thankful I did not send them. I guess I keep them to remind myself how important it is to be slow to react to a situation.

Getting it off your chest and putting it in writing is very cathartic. Along the same line, why not spout off about whomever on your way home, knowing full well you would not think of saying it to their face? Then when you get home, leave all those issues in the car. As a matter of fact, you just might find a reasonable solution to the issues by talking it out with no one else around.

Therefore, when you walk in the door any events your children are experiencing should not create a crisis for you. They are merely events with consequences. Consequences do not require emotional involvement by any one, save the actual participant. If you didn't cause it, why fix it? That sounds rather mercenary but, number one – if a child never learns to *fix* what he *broke*, how is he going to learn responsibility? Secondly, you must ask yourself what are rights that every child should have and what are privileges?

Rights involve the following: Every child has a right to be loved, properly fed, clothed, sheltered and educated. Anything less is abuse. Anything beyond is a privilege. For example: A child has a right to be educated, but if he misses the bus because he slept in – it is not your fault unless, of course, you were the one who kept him up late. This is a golden opportunity to teach responsibility and accountability.

Your child has the right to be sheltered, but if she slams her bedroom door so hard it breaks because she was angry with you or someone else, that isn't your problem. It's hers. This is a good time to learn to say to her, "I'm sorry you did that; how do you intend to fix it?"

Getting angry does not help. Hitting does not help. Saying nothing does not help. Holding her accountable does. And if she refuses to respond in a reasonable length of time, remove the door. It usually doesn't take long before teenagers will beg to have a door again. However, you must make them responsible.

The important thing in all of this is to help the child maintain her self-esteem. Let me give you a personal example.

A few years back I purchased a used Jeep Cherokee.

This is the vehicle that was advertised by Chrysler as the machine "you never want to loan to anyone to whom you gave birth." The message of this ad was clear – your child will test the limits of every function of the vehicle. This includes *take off* from zero to 60, stopping distance, how steep a hill it will climb, what angle it takes to roll over, and much, much more.

But how are you going to keep it away from them without standing guard? This is especially true when your son says to you, "Dad, it sounds like the brakes are bad. Why don't you take something else to work and I'll fix the brakes?"

Since my 17-year-old son had a wonderful aptitude for mechanics, had all the necessary tools, and could save me driving 50 miles to a repair shop, I left the Cherokee at home with the offer to pay him for his troubles.

With snow-packed roads, it was important that the brakes didn't malfunction in some fashion causing me to slide into a ditch. So I was grateful that Craig had taken an interest in our *new-to-us* four-wheel drive.

Since the sun set so early, it was after dark when I arrived back home. Not paying any particular attention to the Jeep that was parked outside facing away from me, I went in the house to see how things went. I asked him about the brakes. He responded that they were all replaced and worked perfect. I paid him for the parts and for his labor, for which he seemed especially grateful.

I was rather surprised at his attentiveness to me that evening and somewhat elated that he was concerned about my well-being and my day at work. Then came a moment of silence. Almost as if he was unloading a big weight off his chest he said, "I smashed the front of the Jeep." As if to minimize the impact of the statement he continued, "All the brakes locked up at the same time, so you don't have to worry about one grabbing."

Sure enough, Craig had hit the crusted snow bank at the end of the road head on. The imprint of the grill, bumper and headlights were in perfect reflection on the snow. Glass from the headlights was still embedded in the snow bank.

I assured him that I was impressed with his brake job, but was curious as to how he was going to fix the front of the car. "I can get used parts at the junk yard and, with any luck, I can get white to match our paint," he responded. Within two weeks the car was back in shape as if nothing had happened.

That was his accident and his problem – therefore, I had no reason to be upset. It would have done me little good to ban him from driving for six months, send him to his room, refuse to pay him for his work or storm off to care for the injured car myself. I got what I needed from him and he, in turn, learned a lesson.

Giving a child the right to respond and offer to fix the problem without a parent overreacting does wonders for relationships. Sometimes, because of age or other factors, it might be impossible for them to fix or resolve a problem. That is when you negotiate a deal. You'll take care of their problem if they will do something for you. My daughter learned how to mow the lawn and wash cars through such negotiations.

One final thing in this chapter which is important for you to consider: Generally, anger is the result of an unmet expectation. You expect something from your child that didn't happen. The classic response is to get their attention by way of anger, bursts of yelling or the threat of punishment. I am not suggesting you reduce your expectations if they are reasonable. What I am proposing is offering your child the respect of a human being and respond with a different strategy than what is customary for you. Stretch the limits of your possibilities in parenting by trying a new venture from this book that you have never thought of doing previously.

REVIEW

■ If it isn't your fault, why get upset? If it is your fault, why blame the child?

■ Change the mistakes your child makes into "teachable moments" rather than a time to release your own pent up frustrations.

■ Getting even is not a right a parent has.

■ Improve relationships by giving your child the right to respond and a chance to fix the problem.

■ Consequences do not require emotional involvement on the part of the parent.

■ Be certain you understand clearly the difference between rights and privileges.

■ If you didn't cause it, why fix it? That is the responsibility of the one who broke it.

■ Compromise is a good thing. The goal is generally reached sooner and easier.

■ Transferring your emotions from work on to your children is unfair.

■ Unmet expectations can be the primary cause of anger.

IF PARENTING IS A THREE RING CIRCUS, HOW COME I'M NOT THE RINGMASTER?

CHAPTER SEVEN

Illogically speaking

Why not go out on a limb?

Isn't that where the fruit is?

— FRANK SCULLY

Swallow hard and try to get through this before you pass judgment. I am about to say something you might not like. Here it is. Ready?

IF LOGIC DOESN'T WORK, WHY USE IT?

I know this statement sounds more like an oxymoron than anything else, but there is a mountain of truth in it.

A gentleman came into my office one day for some help. He was a…. I won't get into his profession. Let me just say he was a concrete operational thinker and *logic* was the king of his life.

His first comment to me was, "I want you to fix my wife."

"What's wrong with her?" I asked.

"She is so illogical it is disgusting. I try to explain things to her and show her how to organize the house, but she just won't listen. What seems to create the greatest argument is when I let her drive. Frankly, I don't know how she keeps from killing herself without me along telling her about other traffic and what she needs to do to keep from getting into an accident. As a matter of fact, it is so bad, our marriage is in a downward spiral."

"I can't 'fix' her, but you can," I responded. "As a matter of fact, it's a simple little phrase I learned a long time ago that can make the difference between happiness and sorrow."

"I suppose you are going to tell me that a little phrase is going to solve my marriage problems," he responded sarcastically.

"Not really. It is what you do with the phrase that is going to make the difference," I retorted.

"Okay, let's have it. I am so desperate I am willing to try almost anything."

"You might not like it but here it is. 'If logic doesn't work – don't use it.'"

It was almost as if I had slapped him across the face. "That is the most idiotic, senseless, and hair-brained thing I have ever heard in my life. 'If logic doesn't work – don't use it,'" he mimicked. "That's impossible!"

I smiled, which caught him off guard. He was expecting an argument.

"What?" he queried.

"So tell me, has any of your logic helped your marriage relationship?" I asked. "After all, you confessed that you argue in the car, she won't speak to you at home and even finds ways to avoid being in your presence. So tell me, is what you are doing working?

"No," was his cryptic response.

"Now, that is the 'most idiotic, senseless and hair-brained thing I have ever heard in my life,'" I repeated back to him. "It just doesn't make sense to continue a pattern of thought if it isn't endearing your wife to you and bringing you happiness."

To assure him he was not alone in this boat that wasn't going anywhere, I shared a story about my wife and me.

I was in a hurry to get to the airport. Not wanting to pay the parking fee at the airport since I was going to be gone for several days, I asked Bonnie if she would take me. I asked her to drive so I could just hop out and get in line at the ticket counter.

Busying myself in the car to make certain I had everything, I failed to notice the direction Bonnie was heading. I don't quite remember what prompted me to look up but when I did, I realized she was taking a different route to the airport. Fortunately, she was still headed in the right direction.

I did ask her where she was going, just to make sure. "To the airport," she responded.

"Maybe this is a way to the airport but it is not the quickest way," I retorted in exasperation.

She kept driving her way. I began to extol the virtues of going the other direction in logical terms. Because of my frustration, I am certain that my para-verbal communication was a bit tense. My tone was higher pitched, my volume was louder, and the speed of my sentences was faster than normal. She insisted her way was the quickest, and I argued the opposite.

"Isn't it amazing," I told the gentleman sitting in front of me, "that husbands and wives never really argue about serious issues? It is usually about things that don't really matter in the long run." I continued my illustration.

In the midst of all of this contention she smiled at me.

"What?" I responded tersely. Her smile was so spontaneous. It confused me, and I couldn't help responding by saying, "What?"

"Would you rather be right or happy?" she asked. Of course, I wanted to be right and happy. "No, no," she said. "If you could only choose one, which would it be?"

It was very difficult to answer because I wanted to be right so badly that I didn't want to admit that I would rather be happy.

Our trip the rest of the way to the airport was in silence.

"Silence," I said to the gentleman, "is our way of standing before the court and admitting 'no contest.'"

After mulling my dilemma over in my mind for the two hours on the plane, I came to the realization that happiness is far more important than being right. Being right is not one of mankind's strongest traits of character. Therefore, it is the better part of wisdom to be happy.

It took some time, but my friend finally mastered the philosophy.

Lest you think this idea is way out in left field, let me assure you that Jesus used this approach numerous times. One of the classics is found in Luke 5. Here's how the story transpires.

Everywhere Jesus went there was a crowd of people. This particular day the crowd was exceptionally heavy and anxious to get close to Jesus. So much so that Jesus found himself right on the shores of Lake Gennesaret. If the people didn't quit crowding him, he would have to start walking on water. But rather than do that, which would have really distracted the people, he turned to Simon Peter, who was washing his nets after a wasted night of fishing. There wasn't anything more in their nets than plant life. Not one hint of a fish was to be found.

Jesus stepped into Peter's boat and asked him if he would push out a little ways from the land. The Bible doesn't say how long he spoke, but when he was done, as a gratuity to Peter for letting him use his boat, he told him to go a bit further out and cast out his nets.

Peter was no dummy. He knew full well that if you don't catch fish at night, you certainly aren't going to catch them during the day when the sun is beating down on the water. Logically speaking, it was going to be a waste of their time. They had pulled the nets in just before the break of dawn, had just finished cleaning them when Jesus asked to use their boat, and now Jesus was asking them to throw them out again. This meant washing the nets all over again before nightfall. It just didn't make sense and Peter expressed that. Here is my rendition of what Peter would have said if this experience had happened today.

"Lord, throwing in our nets doesn't make sense. We worked all night trying to catch something, but the waters were so barren we didn't even get so much as a tear in our nets. There is absolutely no logic in this. However, since you asked, I'll do it."

Peter knew enough about Jesus he was willing to do this only because Jesus asked. But in his professional opinion, it was a waste of time. The Bible records the biggest catch they ever had. So much so they had to call James and John out to help them.

Isn't it just like many sons today? They take Dad's boat out and almost swamp it, break the nets, and leave just as soon as they hit land leaving everything for the fathers to clean up, fix up and, may I add, to their credit – collect the revenue, because the four young men weren't interested in fishing anymore. Anymore, that is, until later on when they got a bit discouraged.

This time it was after Jesus' death and resurrection. Several of the disciples were with Peter at the Sea of Tiberius. Melancholy had set in and they were just sitting around brooding. Peter, anxious to do anything, declares he is going fishing. John 21 records the event.

All night they are out on the sea with absolutely no results. There is nothing worse than failing at the very thing you were hoping would buoy up your spirits. Maybe it was because Thomas and Nathaniel were along. They were novices, at best, at fishing.

Dawn was about to break in its full splendor. They could see a form on the shore, but couldn't identify him. To make matters worse, this person called them "children." They were polite to him anyway and confessed they had a bad night as they continued to struggle to get the net back into the boat. That is when the figure called out, "Throw your net over the other side."

It had been three years since Peter had first learned that logic doesn't always work. Since that time he watched and heard that philosophy over and over again. He heard Jesus tell the story of the prodigal son (Luke 15). For the majority of those listening to the story it was totally illogical for a father whose son had wasted a third of his estate to hold a banquet reserved typically for visiting royalty. Many of those listening sided with the older brother, but not if you were a father whose son had disappeared. Not if that son is the *apple of your eye*. A father soon forgets all the trouble there ever was. His eyes would tell the tale of hours, days and perhaps years, of worry and speculation over the fate of that son, and he wants to say "I love you" one more time.

When Jesus began the speech with the parable of the lost sheep, he asked: "If you had one hundred sheep, and one of them strayed away and was lost in the wilderness, wouldn't you leave the ninety-nine others to go and search for the lost one, until you found it?" (Luke 15:4 NLT)

For the crowd of wealthy Pharisees and scribes listening, the logical answer to that question is, "No, I wouldn't." They're businessmen; a one-percent loss in a given year is excellent. Shepherds can stand to lose three to five percent and still make money. Besides, who would think of risking their life to chase after a wandering sheep that might already have been attacked and killed? Who would be so stupid to risk their entire flock to marauders, wolves, bears and the like just for one careless sheep that weighed more than you could have thought of carrying? It's just not fiscally responsible or logical. Only a shepherd who knows all his sheep by name would bypass logic.

That was exactly the point. Jesus would do it for any man lost in the clutches of sin. He would risk everything – even his life. In contrast to the Pharisees and scribes the publicans and sinners listening welcomed this ray of hope into their lives.

This whole scenario is reminiscent of a comment the Lord made in the Old Testament. "Can a mother forget her nursing child? Can she feel no love for a child she has borne? But even if that were possible, I would not forget you!" (Isaiah 49:15 NLT)

This time there was no hesitation on Peter's part. He knew that faith and hope could come in the narrow quarters between starboard and port. And, indeed, it did. The ensuing results compelled John to declare, "It is the Lord."

Logic should never be the point. Love is. Forgiveness is. Valuing another person is.

Here's another twist that might be helpful. I have a Chinese classic entitled *The Art of Warfare* by Sun Tzu. Since Americans use it as a book on business strategy, there are a few things that are appropriate for leadership in the home and family. Listen to this and think about how well it fits:

"The traits of the true commander are: wisdom, humanity, respect, integrity, courage and dignity. With his wisdom he humbles the enemy, with his humanity he draws the people near to him, with his respect he recruits men of talent and character, with his integrity he makes good on his reward, with his courage he raises the morale of his men, and with his dignity he unifies his command." (Page 226)

Now that is a healthy approach to a relationship that allows you to maintain your respect and authority. Children and adults alike don't need the cruelty that is sometimes derived from egocentric logic and the demand for respect. They need to experience the adventure and hope of acceptance regardless of how ridiculous their actions.

The definition of insanity is "doing the same thing over and over again and expecting different results."

REVIEW

- If logic doesn't work, don't use it.

- Being right is not as important as being happy. If someone wants to prove you wrong, they will.

- Logic should never be the point of an argument. Love and forgiveness should be the focal points.

IF PARENTING IS A THREE RING CIRCUS, HOW COME I'M NOT THE RINGMASTER?

CHAPTER EIGHT

Discipling is not a spectator sport

The delight we inspire in others has this enchanting peculiarity. That, unlike any other reflection, returns to us more radiant than ever. —
VICTOR HUGO

And you yourself must be a good example to them by doing good deeds of every kind. Let everything you do reflect the integrity and seriousness of your teaching. — TITUS 2:7 NLT

I am referring to the real need to disciple (teach) children by getting them involved. The problem with television is that it is not interactive. Children are merely spectators and not participants. They *watch* and *watch* and *watch* and don't get to *do*.

When I was a child, I had to stand around while my father worked on automobiles and farm machinery just in case he needed a tool. Then I could be his errand boy. Otherwise, standing and watching him made little sense, and I learned very little except for one thing. I learned if I didn't bring him the correct tool or, if it took me longer to find it than expected, I would get a whipping for wasting his time.

Reminiscing about those childhood days, my sister complained that she didn't know a thing about cars and should have paid more attention when she was younger. This is what she wrote in 1994 about her husband, Bruce:

"We've decided that when we buy a new car, we're going to keep both of the others, too, so we'll have at least two to drive in case one breaks down. That's what I get for having my nose in a book while all the rest of you were learning about cars and stuff. The only thing I remember about those days is the profanity. I didn't want to take the chance and hand Dad the wrong tool. You know, even mild-mannered Bruce swears when he's handed the wrong thing.

"I don't know why men can't work on things without having someone around to hand them stuff. I don't make him stand around and hand me things when I hang a curtain or mop the floor. Can you imagine making Bruce come down to the basement with me and when I get the clothes in the washer I say, 'Bruce, will you hand me the detergent now? No! Not the fabric softener, you idiot!'"

I have news for her. We didn't learn because our father showed us what to do. We learned because if it broke down when we were using it, he would blame us. So, we learned mechanics by default.

There are several key components to discipling that Jesus portrayed very effectively.

He never reprimanded those who wanted to learn.

He gave clear instructions and then sent them out to practice on their own.

He never revealed any of the dark secrets he knew about any of them. What he knew about Judas, no one else knew.

He gave them a chance. He gave them responsibility.

He saw possibilities when no one else could. For most people, these disciples were lowly Galileans. To Jesus, they were the key to spreading the Gospel.

He led them and left them with hope.

One vital factor in discipling is encouraging your child to become what they want to be rather than what you want them to be. Too many parents try to steer their children in the career similar to their own, or attempt to persuade them into becoming someone different than what they were made up to be.

History is replete with people who were forced into being someone they were not. One of the classics in this case was Isaac Watts. Although Watts is seen today as the most prolific composer of hymns (over 600 in total), his childhood was disastrous on many counts. Even though his father was an independent thinker himself, he did not give the same freedom to Isaac, the oldest of his nine children. Isaac began learning Latin at age four and was so fascinated with languages that he also learned Greek, Hebrew and French.

What irritated Isaac's father more than anything was Isaac's incessant rhyming when he spoke. His father was quite annoyed at this and continually badgered Isaac to stop speaking in verse. Isaac couldn't stop. He couldn't help himself. It was too big a part of who he was. Once his father started to whip him, thinking Isaac could stop if he wanted to, whereupon young Isaac declared as his father struck the first blow,

"O father, do some pity take
And I will no more verses make."

Florence Nightingale is another figure in history who went against her family's wishes. The daughter of wealthy parents, she was privileged to live a life of ease, opulence and comfort. Why Florence came to want to be a nurse will remain a mystery. But one thing we do know is that nurses in those days were considered about as low on the status level as you could get.

After little more training than a modern day first-aid class, she headed to the front lines of the Crimean War. Within six months she had reduced the death rate in the field hospitals from 42 percent to 22 percent. She also single handedly changed the perception of nursing to a respectable profession. In spite of a heart condition she lived to 90 years of age.

I guess the bottom line to discipling is – you need to consider that your child will, one day, be an adult, barring any tragedies. What they bring into adulthood is an accumulation of experiences and wonderment from childhood. What experiences do you really want to last? Do you want them to grow up fearing you, hating you, living a miserable life because they aren't doing anything related to their inward passion? The more positive experiences a person learns as a child, the less apt they are to get into trouble as a teen or an adult. And these experiences don't necessarily have to be related to who they wish to become as an adult. They only have to give a child the idea that they are worth something, and the experiences, regardless of how hard they may be, can have successful endings.

Building assets is critical. The more they have the better they will feel about themselves. Here are a few examples: hobbies, interests, a value of self (self worth), responsibilities – like chores, etc.

It is never too late to provide a young person with an approach to life that will change his life. An elderly gentleman whom I greatly admired reminded me over and over again that I continually needed to create events that cause kids to rally.

I will never forget a call I received one day from a juvenile probation officer during the years we were doing specialized foster care placements. His first comments to me were, "We have a 14-year-old shoplifter who can't seem to keep his hands off things in stores. We have arrested him so many times we have lost count. We finally resorted to putting him in detention. He lives with his grandmother, and she is heart broken. We have called you to see if you can find a place for this young man out of our county. Maybe different scenery will help him."

"I don't think it's the scenery," I responded. "What I really want to know is: What are his hobbies and interests. What has he done or seen done before that he would like to do again? What has he never done before that he would love to try?"

"That's pretty ridiculous," the probation officer retorted. "What does that have to do with his criminal activity and inappropriate behavior?"

"An awful lot," was my immediate reply. "You get the answers to these questions, and I'll do my best to help you."

A couple days later I heard back from the probation officer. "He says he has always wanted to fly airplanes. He claims he would 'die' to live around them."

Within a couple weeks I had located a home with a family that was surrounded with airplanes. There were wrecked airplanes, airplane parts and pieces and, of course, airplanes that looked brand new. Of course, there was a runway connected to the pasture where these planes were tied down.

To be sure, there were some initial challenges until this young man learned the rules of the house, the shop and the graveyard of airplane parts. Once he learned those he was about the happiest young man you could find. Not once after moving into that home did he experience a shoplifting adventure.

I know it's work, but you can find something that will make your adventure into the world of your child worthwhile. Go ahead; make your child's life great. See what a difference an interest or hobby will make.

REVIEW

- Teaching children is far better than just making them watch.

- Encourage your child to become what they want to be rather than what you expect of them.

- Help strengthen your child's interests even if they aren't your interests. Find a mentor if necessary. This will go a long way in reducing a teen's interest in drugs, crime and poor friends.

IF PARENTING IS A THREE RING CIRCUS, HOW COME I'M NOT THE RINGMASTER?

CHAPTER NINE
The gentle enforcer

The game of life is the game of
boomerangs. Our thoughts, words
and deeds return to us sooner or later
with astounding accuracy.
— *FLORENCE SHINN*

Simply put: "You must say what you mean, mean what you say, and don't be mean about what you say." Any rule you put out should not be for show but for enforcement. So, the key points are that the rules should be easily understandable, short and to the point. And, finally, what you say must be enforceable.

You don't tell a teenager that he cannot watch television and then leave him alone for the evening. If he hadn't figured it out before, he will, just as soon as you leave.

Here's one that we have dealt with more than once. The parents want to take a vacation without the children. Since they are all over 12, the parents leave on a two-week vacation with clear instructions that the children are not to have anyone over, and there are to be no parties while they are gone.

Any guess as to how long it takes for the average teenager to invite their friends over once parents are out of sight? The invitees are called that day with a date for the party the next day (that's to be certain that the parents won't be coming back because they forgot something). One other thing the *poor* home-alone children will do is make certain there are no parties happening at the time you said you were going to call every day.

So, the key is not to order anything that you cannot enforce.

The biggest challenge in life is staying consistent. In many cases the degree of a teenager's rebelliousness is in direct proportion to how inconsistent the rules were during early childhood. It behooves all of us to be reminded of what the writer of the Book of Hebrews said about Jesus: "the same yesterday, and today, and forever". (Hebrews 13:8 NLT)

To be certain, there are times when it is best to bend the rules because of a particularly important event. But that should be the exception rather than the rule. What I am talking about are the rules changing based upon the disposition of the parent.

A case in point is when a parent has been angry with their child over an unrelated incident and then feels remorseful and wants to be accommodating. This is when a youngster realizes the opportunity to get something he wants but normally can't have. He knows better than to ask for anything related to the incident, so he will ask for something totally unrelated.

Supposing your house rule is that your teen cannot take the car out after dark. But the day before, you and your child got into a big fight over the use of the telephone. You overreacted and did and said some things you shouldn't have. So today you are feeling really bad about it and apologize. Your child forgives you with open arms. You are so relieved they are willing to forgive you. This is when you need to be careful.

Your child will use this occasion as a golden opportunity to circumvent another rule. The next thing you know the child is asking for permission to use the car "just to run over to a friend's house for a few minutes." They try to minimize the rule infraction and convince you that it is just compensation for their forgiveness. Many parents cave at this point and say, "Well, okay. But don't be long."

The parent is trying to avoid another altercation so soon after the other has been mended. Thinking that this break in the rule will help mend the relationship further, they give in. What the parent doesn't realize is that once the teen is out of sight they roll down the window of the car and yell, "Sucker!" as loud as they can. Okay, maybe they don't yell it, but they realize they have your number, and it isn't unlisted either.

Kids are smart. Next time they want to use the car after dark, they will do one of two things. They will either sabotage the relationship the day before so you will overreact and then have to apologize, or they will be a bit more brazen and just point blank ask you – having, as ammunition, your previous laxness in maintaining the rule.

A case in point is a family who had a very definite rule that their children were not to use alcohol and tobacco. Good rule. But their 15-year-old daughter found a way around that rule. She had gotten hooked on cigarettes at school. To be in the *socially elite*, she *had* to smoke. Unfortunately, when she got hooked, she got really hooked.

At times her evening craving for a cigarette was so bad that she had to figure a way to have one without her parents knowing anything about it. There wasn't a problem when her parents were gone for the evening, but when they had no place to go, and she *needed a cigarette*, she had to take drastic action. Her plan worked out better than she could have ever imagined. She picked a fight with her parents.

The arguments became so intense she would storm out of the house, slam the door and rush behind the shop that was on the property. The parents told me they were so relieved she was gone, they never checked to see where she went for fear of getting into another altercation. They weren't really worried about her running away because she would always come back within an hour, march right past them, and go to bed.

It took them six months to catch on to what was happening. That is why I said earlier in this book that you have to stay awake at night trying to think of ways to outsmart your very own children. Some parents, disturbed at their child's behavior, reminisce about how bad they were when they were teenagers. They are always quick to interject that they were "never as bad as this." This is when I remind them the word "diaper" spelled backwards is "repaid."

Enforceable rules must be fair. Being fair does not always mean being equal. What works for one doesn't work for another. What appeals to one doesn't appeal to the other. The majority of young people who come to Project PATCH have grown up with ineffective and senseless rules, or rules that were either too rigid or too flexible. Oh, and there is one other key ingredient to a good rule. There must be a good reason for it – beyond having one just because "I said so." If you can't or won't enforce a rule, then eliminate it. Both you and the child will feel much better.

A few years back there were four young men at our Project PATCH Ranch who had more energy than they had day left. They were four among 15 who had been outside playing soccer. When the game was over and it was time to go back to the dorm, these particular four boys asked if they could stay outside a bit longer. It was early May and one of the first really warm days of the year.

The dorm director responded by saying, "If you want to stay out a bit longer, why not make yourselves useful? Take the canoe out of storage and set it on the bank of the pond." The pond was less than 200 feet from the storage shed. Only a ten-foot-wide dike and dam separated the river and the pond. The rule was: No canoe or rowboat was to be put in the river for any reason because of the swift current and Class III and IV rapids.

The dorm director and the other staff were busy with the 11 other teens, and trusting that the four would soon be in, forgot to check on them. About a half hour later we received a call from a neighbor down river. His first comment surprised me a bit. "I think we have four of your boys down here below my house on the river bank."

"What makes you think they are our boys?" I asked incredulously.

"Because they are loud, boisterous, and think they have just conquered the world. Besides, they are soaking wet."

"Must be our boys," I responded. "But I'll check the boys' dorm to make certain." Sure enough, four were missing, and the staff was just beginning to fan out to look for them. I assured them that I knew where they were and took a couple staff members down to check things out. Sure enough, they were the four that had been asked to take the canoe to the pond.

They all wanted to talk at once about their harrowing adventure. What I got from each of their interrupted and excited comments was this. They were taking the canoe to the pond when one ventured the challenge of going for a canoe ride down the river. Four boys, two paddles and no life jackets. Since no one was looking their direction, they slipped into the water and were gone out of sight in short order.

They only meant to go a short distance, they claimed. But with the current being so swift and having so much fun, they thought they would make the best of their adventure. Things were going well for them until they hit a bend in the river with a set of rapids. They hit a rock in the middle of the river, which buckled the canoe into a horseshoe. Unceremoniously thrown out, they struggled against the current to reach shore. The canoe, on the other hand, weaseled its way away from the rock and continued down river.

Grateful that they were all alive, the staff felt that since it was getting late in the day, the boys should change their clothes, eat and rest up, which meant, "We will talk about it in the morning."

I pulled the staff aside as the boys were climbing the bank to get into the van and told them that waiting was not a good idea. In order for consequences to be effective, anything we did must be immediate. The boys might consider it punitive retribution the next morning.

"What do you suggest?" they asked.

"First they get dry clothes on, and then they go find the canoe. We won't tell them the rest of it until the canoe is found," I responded.

Once we got back to the dorm and they were all in dry clothes, I announced that we were going to look for the canoe. "Why?" was their response. "It's toast."

"Because the canoe didn't belong to you, and because you lost it."

We drove them back to the area where they lost the canoe. We all got out and started walking the riverbank. I wanted to make certain they didn't get into any more trouble.

"What if the canoe is clear down at Black Canyon Dam?" one of the boys asked.

"Then we will walk the 50 miles to Black Canyon Dam or until we find the canoe," I said cheerfully. "Beside, we're all in this with you. We'll all feel better with a long walk."

We walked along the riverbank until there was no longer a bank and the terrain was steep. The road was now over a hundred feet above the river. We spotted the canoe lodged between a rock and the steep bank.

Time was of the essence. Evening shadows were playing with the branches of the trees. "There it is, boys," I yelled. "Go get it."

"We'll die," they declared in all seriousness. True, it was a steep bank but it wasn't so steep that it would put them in any serious danger. It would take some energy to get down there and much more energy to get back up.

"I'll watch," I said. "You young men didn't seem to care much about your life a couple hours ago by going down this treacherous river with no life jackets, and in a canoe at that. So I am certain you are brave enough to go down this embankment."

One at a time they stepped over the guardrail and began sliding down the bank, catching trees and bushes on their descent.

An important factor in following through with your mission of staying firm to your commitment is not to buy into other distractions that young people will try to fling your way. If a teen questions your intelligence, contends that your lineage takes a different ancestral path than most humans, says something bad about your mother, or even that your facial features are uglier than different parts of one's anatomy – stay focused. Those comments are only to get you distracted from the issue and have absolutely no substance in reality.

Remember, it is not your problem – it's theirs. You do not have to become defensive. Stay on the offensive. Stay calm, which will irritate them even more for a few moments. When they realize they aren't getting to you, their loud comments and gestures will wane to a grumble and then to silence.

One rule that was established on the spot was that they all participated in the loss, so therefore, they all had to participate in bringing it back to the road.

It was dark before they made it to the safety of the road, and they were relieved that they were done with this escapade. Their immediate reaction was to try to put the canoe in the back of the pickup that appeared to be waiting in anticipation to receive their burden.

Before they were lucky enough to hoist it into the pick-up, I stopped them. "Wait, it doesn't go in the back of the pickup."

"How are you going to get it back to the Ranch?" they asked in unison.

"What were you told to do in the first place?" They looked puzzled. "You know – about four o'clock this afternoon?"

"You mean – 'take the canoe to the pond?'" They asked quizzically.

"Exactly. It is not my fault the canoe is now five miles further away from the pond. So you fellows start walking with the canoe, and we will follow along behind with the pickup."

It took them three hours to reach the pond. Oh, they could have made it sooner, but we stopped every half hour and gave them snacks and drinks and had a little five-minute party.

You see, if you do it right, and you don't buy into any verbal attacks on your character, you can help a young person through their torturous consequence. The key is to stick to it. They will be better off for it, and you might not have to repeat it again, as was true in this case.

The next morning I met the young men with a smile as if nothing serious had happened the night before. They were sitting together nursing their blisters. "Hey fellows, would you like to do that again?" I asked cheerfully.

"Not a chance," they grumbled. "The trip down the river was a blast, but hauling that stupid canoe back to the pond was torture."

See what I mean? They were cured. And your child can be too. It is never too late to reestablish your limits. Your children might be shocked at first, but don't worry, they'll get over it and come out the better for it.

REVIEW

- Enforceable rules must be fair.

- Being fair is not synonymous with being equal.

- Insisting on anything you cannot or will not enforce is a dead-end street. "Say what you mean, mean what you say and don't be mean about it."

- There must be a good reason for a rule. Regardless of how good you think a rule is, if you don't follow through with it, then eliminate it.

- Delaying any consequence is not healthy. It merely breeds contempt.

- Regardless of what names a child calls you, what they say about your lineage, looks, intelligence, or body odor – stay focused on the issue. Later, when the issue has been resolved you can research the validity of those charges.

IF PARENTING IS A THREE RING CIRCUS, HOW COME I'M NOT THE RINGMASTER?

CHAPTER TEN

Cheering them on

Look beneath the surface; let not the several quality of a thing nor its worth escape thee.
— *MARCUS AURELIUS ANTONIUS*

I praise loudly; I blame softly.
— *CATHERINE THE GREAT*

Compliments are an asset in strategizing a victory over your child's purposeful rebellion.

We all thrive on compliments. Compliments have a way of boosting the ego and endearing the recipient to the donor. Compliments should either be the introduction or part of the discipline equation. The following story describes what could have happened as opposed to what actually happened.

Esther was a lovely lady with a disturbing secret. She felt she had ruined the bond between herself and her son. I am certain it was nothing intentional on her part, but what she did was, to her, a matter of pride and principle.

Her son, Jeff, came bounding down the stairs – late as usual for breakfast and the school bus. It wouldn't be long before the squeak of brakes would beckon him to the awaiting yellow bus. But this morning, life was going to take a turn for the worse in just a matter of a couple of minutes.

As Jeff charged towards the table ready to consume the array of food Mom had just fixed for him, Esther momentarily took her eyes off her kitchen chores to take that regular morning glance at Jeff to see if he was dressed properly for school. After all, Jeff's parents were well known in the community, and for Mom, how Jeff dressed for school was a matter of personal pride.

She glanced and thoughtlessly turned away only to be jerked back into the reality of what she had just seen on Jeff. Jeff knew better, Mom thought, so why was he testing the waters? It was almost too late to argue, but for Mom it was necessary.

Jeff had started life that morning with a split in the inseam of the left pant leg. It extended from his crotch to his knee. "Jeff, go upstairs and change those pants before you miss the bus," Mom said flatly, trying to hide her frustration.

"Mommmm, all the kids are wearing clothes like this. Besides, I am 15 years old, and it's about time I got to wear what I wanted to wear once in a while." Jeff seemed to be determined in his defiance. So Mom upped the ante a bit, thinking this would solve the problem.

"You go take those pants off, or I'll take them off for you." Ooops. She made a strategic error. What if he called her bluff? Jeff was no small child anymore. He was pressing six foot and 175 pounds. But the die had been cast. Was he going to be the obedient child of yesteryear or was he going to rebel?

"You and whose army?" Jeff retorted.

"Dad, come in here," Esther demanded. Dad had been in the garage and was ignorant of this interchange until the tone in Esther's voice told him he had better report for duty quickly.

Poor Dad was in a pickle. If he sided with the son, he was in serious trouble for a long, long time. If he sided with Mom, then he had to force Jeff into a position of acceptance to their authority on this issue.

Dad gave Jeff one last chance. "Either take those pants off, or we'll take them off for you." Both Mom and Dad knew they either had to act or lose this battle and, perhaps, others for good.

"Make me," was Jeff's stubborn reply. In an instant the once calm house turned into pandemonium. Mom and Dad attacked with lightning speed and like a well oiled machine. Dad went for the upper arms and Mom went for the belt to release the offending pants from their grasp around the waist. Little did they realize that Jeff would respond with the fury of a bobcat.

When the battle was over, Dad's clothes were ripped and Mom was almost totally disrobed. But they did get the pants off, only to see them retrieved by Jeff as he stormed out the back door, cursing and vowing never to step foot in that house again.

As Esther sat across from me sharing the details of this tragic story, tears ran down her cheeks like a water faucet. She wanted to know if she was right and how to mend the broken relationship. "What could I have done differently?" she sobbed.

"It's too late for that incident," I declared. "But it is important for you to find your son and apologize to him."

"Why?" she stammered. "He was being disobedient."

"Maybe so," I said. "But was a split in the pants more important than a good relationship with your son? Were those pants so important that you were willing to kill a relationship on behalf of your pride?"

"No, I don't suppose so," she replied. "But I still don't think it is proper for him to go to school dressed like that. So what could I have done differently?"

"Unfortunately, you want to know how to close the barn door after the horse is gone," I said. "But for future incidents, let me share a few principles with you that will allow your son to maintain his dignity and you to hold to your standards. Are you ready? This might be tough at first, but with a little practice you will like the concepts."

She nodded.

"The first key component is always to be complimentary. People like to hear genuine compliments.

Plus, it gives you time to think rather than react. What you should have done the minute you saw the offending pants was to say to him, 'My, what beautiful legs you have. They are absolutely gorgeous, and that rip in your pants accentuates their beauty. I'm really afraid for you to get on the bus because, knowing teenage girls like I do, they are going to rip those pants right off of you.'"

Esther ventured a chuckle visualizing the imaginary episode. "He'll just say, 'Bring them on. I can handle it.' That doesn't sound like a very good strategy."

"But, you see, you want to exhaust all his options before you go in for the *kill*. You want him to believe there is an adventure awaiting him if he gets on the bus. Then you say to him. 'That's okay, son. Since I am certain that is going to happen, the minute you get on the bus, I am going to run right up the stairs, grab a pair of decent pants, get in the car and race the bus to school. When I get there I am going to go to the principal and tell him that the girls probably tore your pants off, and I just brought these so he could have you change once you got to school. You wouldn't want to distract all the rest of the girls now, would you?'"

"What would he do if you explained it to him that way?"

"He'd run up stairs and change his pants," she responded.

"Why?" I queried.

"Because the last thing he ever wants to happen is for me to go to his school and embarrass him. I would be an embarrassment to him by just showing up."

"Exactly," I declared. "You will have won the battle by compliments and by a subtle strategy that will help him maintain his own dignity and still accomplish what you want done as well."

REVIEW

- Everyone deserves a compliment which should precede any talk of discipline.

- A good rule of thumb is: If a teen is bigger or faster than you, don't use force. It is a sure way to lose.

- Strategize, strategize, strategize.

- You must ask yourself; "Is this about my own personal pride or prejudice, or is it about my child's well being?" If it is the former, you should think twice before you *pick the fight*.

CHAPTER ELEVEN

Guilty by assumption

*We live thick and are in each other's
way and stumble over one another,
and I think we thus lose some
respect for one another.*
— *HENRY DAVID THOREAU*

*Be kind, for everyone you meet
is fighting a battle.*
— *PLATO*

*True affection will overlook many
mistakes; love will not discern them.*
— *ELLEN G. WHITE*

America's judicial system is based upon the premise of "innocent until proven guilty." For many other nations the reverse is true. It is "guilty until proven innocent." What is worse, however, is the guilt by assumption. I am sure you have heard the phrase *presumed guilty* many times.

Assumptions are based upon theory rather than fact. In other words, you observe an event, that event is verifiable. Based upon your history, your prejudices, a run in with another employee or boss, a conflict with your spouse or your children, or you're just plain feeling out of sorts – you make the event something it wasn't intended to be. Let me give you a couple of examples.

You know this man. You know where he was born. You know he was illegitimate. You know his parents are common folk – his dad is a blue-collar worker. And there is something strange about him. He does things no one else has ever done in your lifetime. Things like healing people, restoring sight to the blind, and making the lame to walk. Lepers are healed and the dead raised to life. Things that specialists in the medical community couldn't solve, he did with a touch of a hand or a spoken word. To top it all off, he turned a funeral procession into a parade of celebration.

You also know that there are prophecies foretelling a coming Messiah and Redeemer. Further, you have been under the tyranny of a cruel and heartless foreign invader for many generations, and frankly you are tired of it.

So this man comes along and changes things a bit. But what really *takes the cake* for you is when he feeds 5,000 men, plus women and children, with five small loaves of bread and two fish. Wow, what an opportunity to overthrow the government of Rome!! No more chuck wagons, no more lousy cooks on the battlefield. You wouldn't even care if you got stabbed with a spear. In a matter of moments you would be healed or resurrected to fight again. Wow! What a show! That would send the Romans packing. They'd run like scared rabbits. You don't really know how all this is going to work out but, who cares? This is the best hope you have had in years to get out of this oppression. John 6:15 records a collusion of men ready to take Jesus by force and set him up as a king. Great idea. Great King! Had more people known about it they would have voted the same way.

So Jesus, trying not to make a scene, sends his disciples one direction, and he slips away quietly up into the mountains. But before daybreak Jesus joins his disciples in their boat, in the midst of a stormy sea, calms the water and gets them to Capernaum faster than they could have rowed.

It is in Capernaum that the mob finally catches up to Jesus. Jesus has to tell them that he isn't here to destroy the Romans, but to save them. He isn't here to set up an earthly kingdom, but a heavenly one, and the bread they really want is from heaven. So, many people leave, never to follow Jesus any more. They lose a golden opportunity because they make an assumption based upon their own personal expectations and desires.

We are all guilty of making assumptions that have the potential of being very destructive.

Jacob seemed to have everything stacked against him from almost the beginning of his life. At two his mother passed away. At five Jacob's dad remarried. What neither Jacob nor his father realized was that this *new mother* resented the intrusion of a five year old upon her new marriage.

Part of the problem was, Dad didn't know how to care for a small boy. He was so wrapped up in his own grief that Jacob was left to raise himself. Jacob rarely took a bath or changed his clothes. Dad didn't seem to notice. So when a new mother came along, there seemed to be instant dislike. She said things to Jacob like: "If it wasn't for you, your mother would still be alive. You look so ugly and smell so bad no one in their right mind would ever want you."

Stepmom promptly sent him to kindergarten. Things didn't go well for Jacob there, either. He was the shy bashful kid everyone liked to pick on. As the years progressed, Jacob felt increasingly insecure. The bullies at school loved to set Jacob up so it looked like Jacob had done something wrong when, in reality, he had nothing to do with it. He was just in the wrong place at the wrong time. Consequently, when Jacob got into trouble at school, and stepmom found out, Jacob got into even more trouble at home.

It wasn't until Jacob reached his teen years and some adults took a special interest in him that he began to blossom and accept himself as a valuable individual.

Equally as sad are the children who are given the basics in life like food, shelter, and clothing, and the parents just assume they can or will grow up on their own. I have known more than a few parents who figure their child is a terrific kid because they are quiet and appear to entertain themselves quite easily. Little do these parents realize that this type of abandonment will cause a child to seek attention and acceptance somewhere else.

I will never forget a father who called me because his 15-year-old daughter had gotten into some serious trouble. He needed help – like the kind someone would describe as *urgent*.

This man was a professional businessman and well respected in his community. Because of his particular business he was also involved in several service clubs. It seemed as if he was never home except on weekends. Those were the times he took to catch up on things he couldn't do at the office. Then there were always his recreational pursuits, which he confessed were necessary to keep his sanity.

Most people wouldn't argue with his high energy and profile, which made him a model in society. One of the telltale signs that there was trouble on the horizon, however, was he had a wife and one (only one) child. After Melinda was old enough to go school, Mom pursued the career goals she had put on hold for six years.

You must understand Mom's desire to be more than just a *mother*. After all, she had her bachelor's degree, and she didn't want those years of education to go to waste. A further rationalization was that her education was expensive, and her school was prestigious. Therefore, she was *entitled* to make a name for herself as well.

"Melinda seemed to be such a pest those early years," both Mom and Dad confessed. "She was always asking questions and wanting to do something with us when we got home from work, but we were just too busy."

They figured she was about 13 when she wasn't *pestering* them any more. To their relief, it was almost as if she had matured and didn't need as much out of them. Melinda spent most of her time in her bedroom when her mom and dad were home.

That was a bad assumption.

As they talked on I could sense a feeling of blame towards Melinda. They seemed incredulous that she could not understand and appreciate that their jobs were to provide the nicest things in life for her. "Why did she have to go and do something so stupid?" Father complained.

The "stupid" thing Melinda did was steal a car. But let me have her father tell you about it.

"I came home late a couple nights ago. I had some meetings to attend. It was about 11:00 pm when I got home. My wife was already in bed. I don't know what possessed me to do it, but I opened the door to Melinda's room just to check in on her. She wasn't there."

"It was almost like it was scripted. At the very moment I realized she wasn't in her bed, the phone rang. It was the police. They had Melinda in their custody. She was being charged with auto theft and driving without a driver's license."

"I was incensed. I woke my wife up, and we headed to the police station. My first thought was, 'how could she embarrass me like this?' I was going to give her a real lecture regardless of who was there."

"True to my personal commitment I began the lecture the minute I saw her. To my surprise, she didn't seem to care. She interrupted me and said, 'Dad, that was the easiest thing I could do. You see, I am joining a gang. This was my initiation night. It was either steal a car or have sex with all the gang members.'"

"I can't tell you how thankful I was, at that moment, that she had stolen a car."

Can you believe it? They wanted us to fix Melinda. Often the young person who is in trouble is not the source of the problem. It is a wrong assumption to believe that.

Wrong assumptions can run the gambit of our life experiences. For example, have you ever had a bad day and no one understood or notices but you? Sure you have. Everyone does. The trouble with adult humans is that we all feel we have a right to have a bad day but no one else does. Illness, argument, lack of sleep, hunger, environmental depression, a chemical imbalance, or a host of other things, either internal or external, might cause your bad day. What you want more than anything else is for people to treat you nice because you deserve it. So why are we so judgmental of other adults or children when they have a bad day, or worse yet, have a good day when we are having a bad one?

My wife, Bonnie, was an excellent early childhood caregiver to our children. When they cried, she used a five-question list to determine the seriousness of the cry. Were they tired, cold, wet, hungry or in pain? The next order of questions related to less tangible issues. Were they scared, angry (did someone steal their toy), lonely, did they want something they couldn't get, or were they spoiled?

Bonnie was also one who never took anything for granted. When our children, or any of the scores of our foster children, came home from school angry because there were conflicts at school, or because she had shrunk or discolored their clothes in the laundry, or just plain wanted to pick a fight, she would ignore them. I mean she really didn't completely ignore them. She just let them spout off while she busied herself in the kitchen fixing them something to eat. And it was usually something they liked.

When she finished, she quietly placed it in front of them while they were still spouting off. They would subconsciously start eating. When they were about finished, Bonnie's question was usually something like this: "Now just what is it that is really upsetting you?" The issue was drastically minimized because there was food in the stomach.

I am sure you have heard that a way to a man's heart is through his stomach. That is also true with most children. You can't settle many issues if the mind has other critical issues to deal with at the same time.

The point of this whole chapter is to challenge you to reevaluate your decision making process by eliminating assumptions from your interaction with other people – especially your family. Then replace it with a better understanding of the internal and environmental factors that just might be affecting a person's attitude or behavior. Better yet, start looking at those issues that make up the way you treat your family. You just might find a way to make changes that causes life to run a whole lot smoother.

REVIEW

■ Wrong assumptions cripple relationships and communication.

■ If you are going to assume anything, assume the best rather than the worst.

■ The key is – never assume anything.

IF PARENTING IS A THREE RING CIRCUS, HOW COME I'M NOT THE RINGMASTER?

CHAPTER TWELVE
Trade secrets of a great ringmaster

*Let us not be content to wait
and see what will happen, but
give us the determination to
make the right things happen.*
— PETER MARSHALL

*Raising teenagers is like
nailing Jell-O to a tree.*
— ANONYMOUS

Ever watch a magician perform their magical sleights of hand? I can be real close and watch intently and still can't figure it out. But those who are experts know just how it happens. Me, I just stand there dumfounded and amazed at how they perform some of those tricks. I know I am not alone because millions of people every year pay to watch those magicians perform.

Ringmasters also have to have a few tricks up their sleeves just in case an act doesn't go as planned. They have to have an alternative plan, an exit plan, and a distraction plan so the show goes on in spite of unforeseen circumstances. The temptation any Ringmaster can fall into is to focus on the tragedy rather than redirect the audience's thinking to the entire program. The audience will focus on what the Ringmaster focuses on. It behooves them to keep their perspective on the entire process. Here's a few examples that might help you keep some tricks up your sleeves to avoid being the victim or the audience rather than the Ringmaster:

Have you ever noticed that your children never tell you all you want or need to know? They can be so cryptic in talking to you, but listen to them talk to a friend on the phone. At those times you just might as well go to a pay phone or use the time up on your cell, because it will be hours before you have access to a land line again. Oh, and the call waiting? You might as well forget that feature functions when your children are on the phone unless, of course, they are expecting a call from another friend. In that case they can go from one call to the next without a moment's interruption.

Back to being cryptic. I have a cartoon called "Zits" taped to my office wall. In this cartoon Mom, Dad and son Jeremy are at the table eating dinner. Above Jeremy's head is an enormous dark and ominous cloud that has everything that is on Jeremy's mind. At that moment Mom intrudes into his potpourri of thoughts to ask, "Jeremy, would it be so hard just to share what's on your mind?"

I am certain if Scott and Borgman, the authors of this cartoon, had given it a second frame, Jeremy would be seen as saying, "Nothing." And that would have been the entire conversation from Jeremy's side.

Here's a scenario I have heard over and over, not only in my home, but also in the homes of countless other parents.

"How was school today?"

There is usually one of two responses: "Fine" or "Lousy."

"What did you do today?"

"Nothing."

"Did you learn anything today?"

"Nope."

"How was your lunch?"

Again there might be one of two responses: "Fine" or "It sucked."

"Anything special you'd like for dinner?"

"Nope."

That answer serves well until you fix something they don't like, and then you get another response like, "Yuk."

The only time you will get a more complete sentence out of your teenager is if you ask them to do something. Then they will make their conversation a one- or two- sentence conversation starting with, "But, Mom" or "Dad." And they usually draw out the vowel sound for emphasis.

So the trade secret that is imperative you use on your children is this: Use the same strategy on them they use on you. You see, they don't think you are smart enough to do that. So it will come as an absolute surprise. They always hear you speak in complete sentences – unless, of course, you're the father. The main thing they hear from Dad is a grunt which means "I heard you," a groan which means "Maybe" or "Go ask your mother because it's too complicated for me to answer," a "hmmm" which means "I guess so," and a growl which means "No."

But let's assume both parents are speaking in complete sentences. Once you have given an assignment and a specific time you want it started and finished, then everything else should be a one-word sentence. That's when your child will impress you with a couple complete sentences themselves.

"Can I call my friend first?"

"Nope."

"Do I have to?"

"Yup."

"Can't Stephanie do it tonight?"

"No."

What your children want to do at this juncture is engage you in a discussion which, in turn, matures into an argument followed by them running to their bedroom, slamming the door and smiling because they got out of it by picking a fight.

Some parents even go so far as getting so frustrated they will declare in exasperation, "Never mind, I'll do it myself."

If you think that is going to place a guilt trip on your child, you have another think coming. If there is any feeble attempt on their part to offer to do it at this point, it is merely to verify that you really meant, "Never mind." Then they can go in peace knowing full well that you have absolved them of their responsibility.

Another critical arena revolves around any questions you might ask your teen. If you don't use the correct word in your question, they are not *lying* to you, they are just answering your question.

In recent years there has been a national public figure that used this artful strategy very effectively until he was caught in his own lie. The only thing I can figure out is that his parents never caught on to his mastery of this art when he was a teen.

Here's an example of something you might be facing right now:

"Are these your cigarettes?"

"No." This answer usually means, "Since you caught me, no." He is ready to declare that they were a direct loan from a friend. They are for a science experiment he has to complete by the end of the week, and he is a part of the experiment. He is not going to tell you that this is a permanent loan with a consumptive clause in the contract that says, "Once the cigarettes are totally consumed by me, the loan is transferred to an outright gift."

"Are you smoking?"

"No." This answer has a tone of incredulousness. "How dare you think I would smoke right in front of you? Of course I am not smoking now, but just as soon as I get out of the house – you bet, I'll light one up."

"So, if you aren't smoking and these aren't your cigarettes, why do you have them?"

"I'm just keeping them for a friend whose parents would ground him if they caught him smoking." Good excuse. His friend is one of his three egos (me, myself and I). He is confessing to you that you probably would ground him if you caught him smoking, but he figures you are too dumb to ask the right questions. At this moment he has to hurry and get his homework done because he is behind. And you, thinking he is serious, let him go.

So, the important thing is to ask all the necessary questions like, "Have you ever, or are going to, in the future, smoke inside any structure or outside anywhere on this planet, or use this tobacco in any way?" Be sure you cover every possibility. Be certain that you don't say, "I don't ever want to catch you smoking." He will make sure of that. You want to be more specific. "The issue is regardless of whether or not you have smoked in the past, you are not to smoke or do drugs of any sort. If you do, there will be consequences."

This brings me to another point: Do not reveal all the consequences. He just might think the consequences are worth the risk. He wouldn't think of telling you any more than what is immediately important for you to know. Keep your strategy secret. If you don't he will brainstorm ways to sabotage your strategic plan. Let me explain by way of an example. This example will include some of the other strategies I have explained earlier in this book as well. But look for this specific rule of engagement.

Paul, at 14, not only acted mean, but also looked like he was always ready for a fight. He came to our youth ranch for a number of reasons, one of which was anger. Whew, this freight train needed to stay on the tracks. It was going to take more than what he got during his previous 14 years. He was a bit bigger than any other young man there at the time. So his size intimidated the rest of the young men at Project PATCH Ranch. So much so that it was difficult for the others to call him on his behavior or attitude.

Paul chose to do his intimidation when no one else was around. His personal encounter with me was 10:00 pm. It was an hour past bedtime, and no one else was on duty except for the night supervision staff who were busy doing something else and did not notice Paul sneak out of his room and bolt out the front door.

Paul's steam engine was headed right towards me as I was walking to my car. The lights from the dorm cast eerie shadows across his tense face. I turned to face him as he stopped close to me. He was so close he would have knocked me over if he expanded his stomach the least little bit.

"What can I do for you, Paul?" was my tentative question.

"You either get me out of here, or I am going to start kicking sheetrock and bustin' windows," he growled menacingly.

This was certainly not a time for me to exercise my authority. We were alone. He was big. I was little. Furthermore it was dark. So I obliged. "Okay, you can go." I was surprised at how calm those words sounded as they came out of my detached lips.

"But it is late. It's actually too late to make any arrangements tonight," I continued. "So, if you promise me that you will behave yourself, which means not breaking anything, intimidating any of the other boys, and following the expectations of the staff, I will get to work on making the arrangements first thing tomorrow morning. It might take me a couple days. Is that okay?"

He was okay with that, and I had gained time.

Notice: From his standpoint I caved in to his demand. From my standpoint I was delaying the encounter for a more suitable time. Further, (now this is important) I did not tell him where he was going because he didn't tell me or ask me about where. He just wanted out of there.

"Now that we are in agreement, are you able to tell me rationally why you want out of here."

"Cause I want to smoke, and I don't want anybody stopping me."

"No, no," I responded. "Give me a rational reason you want out of here."

"This place is okay, I guess. It's just that the rules and the program fit everyone else, but they aren't for me."

"Would it help if we change the program to suit you?" I was fishing for information.

"No, that's not necessary. I just need to leave."

"Okay, we'll make all the arrangements and let you know when we have everything put together."

Having finished our close encounter, he went back to the dorm and went to bed. The next day we started the machinery going to make certain that I lived up to my promise that he could leave. Two days later it was all set.

Our dorm director asked Paul to go out to the shop for a couple minutes. As they walked into the shop, there were five of our male staff there waiting for Paul. Now, now.

Don't get ahead of the story. This isn't the proverbial woodshed.

"This is the day you get to leave," the dorm director said with a smile. Paul grinned. "Do you know where you are going?"

"Home, of course."

"Did anyone tell you you were going home?"

"No, but where else would I go?"

The dorm director smiled as he continued. "You are going up into the mountains for a couple weeks with a couple of staff. Do you want to go peacefully, or do you want us to carry you?"

Paul looked at the group of caring men there to help him through his struggle. He remembered how much he really missed a father in his home.

"I'll go peacefully," he finally responded.

For the next two weeks Paul and two of our staff walked the trails in the National Forest. He came back to the Ranch 20 pounds lighter and bonded to two men who showed him they cared for him.

He stayed for another year as a result.

A child's urgency is not necessarily your immediacy.

Again, if you buy into their anxiety you are doomed. Stay clear. Do not become emotionally involved. Use their urgency as a tool to remind them of their responsibilities. For example, you have asked them to take out the garbage. Week after week you have been getting excuses. If you are the easygoing type, this can happen, and you have been taking out the garbage. (Shame on you if you have). However, you can still salvage this experience and use your easygoing nature to your advantage at this very opportune time.

So your delinquent garbage collector comes rushing up to you and urges you to take him to the school for practice. He is going to be late. He is desperate. He needs your expertise in maneuvering the car to the school with him in it.

At this moment it is important for you to stay calm and firm and say, "You know, there are just so many hours in the day, and so many days in a week. Since I have had to do your chores for you, I have just run out of time, and I don't have any extra time to take you to school."

First comes the shock, then the manipulation, and perhaps demeaning comments. Remember, stay calm, don't *cave in* until you are certain you have a good negotiating tool that assures you the *garbage collector* will be back on duty the very next time garbage pick-up is due.

Your final offer is to assure him if he helps you then you will, in turn, have time to help him out.

Give them a way to escape. That might even mean giving them choices.

You see, it is important for everyone to save face; if you don't make it possible for them to rescue a situation, there will be war. It might be just cold war at first, but you'll know it.

Back to the book, *The Art of Warfare*. Numerous times in this book Sun-Tzu expressed the fact that if the enemy has boxed you in with no way of escape, there is only one thing to do. You must fight to the death. If you box a child in, that is what she will do. So give your child a way to escape by giving choices. Do not say, "You'll either do this, or else." That is not a choice. It is a threat.

One set of choices is, "Would you rather take out the garbage (a simple task) or wash the car (a more time-consuming experience)?" The object is to make the choices compatible with what you want them to do.

We admitted a combative 12-year-old young man to the PATCH Ranch. He knew more bad words than most adults. Since we don't allow cursing in our institution, there are consequences for using those words.

Upon admission this young man was told of the expectations, and for every foul word he spoke, he had to do 50 push ups. Not surprisingly – he cursed at the thought. That was 50 push-ups he was told. He cursed again. That added another 50. He cursed again. Each time with a bit more defiance. The count was now up to 150.

You have to stop that quickly before it gets so large that it is unenforceable. So the staff checking him in almost shouted, "Wait! Before you say another word, I want to give you a choice." The young man paused.

"You can either do the 150 pushups or go out to wilderness for a couple weeks, and then come back in and do the 150 pushups."

The young man thought for a couple minutes and then responded, "When do you want me to start the push-ups?"

It is critical that you do not expect more than a child is capable of comfortably enduring. It took several days to complete his push-ups and other young men got down beside him to encourage him along.

Save some things for the spouse your child will probably marry in the future.

I know. This sounds a bit ridiculous, but I like this strategy very well. Because it absolves you from immediate responsibility. In addition, you must ask yourself, "Is this issue really worth the fight?"

Now, I know each family has different household standards and expectations. Let's take, for example, the most chronic problem most families seem to have – messy teen bedrooms.

You can take the approach of telling your teen his or her mess is their problem as long as it doesn't pour out into the rest of the house, and you can tell them that clean clothes are only available if they arrive, on time, in the laundry room. Or, you can smile and say to them, "You know, it just doesn't seem to make any difference how often I badger you about your bedroom, it always turns up looking like a war zone. So, I have just decided to leave it until you get married, and let your spouse take care of it. Rest assured, life will be much tougher on you unless you get into the habit now."

This one strategy reduces a whole lot of frustration and, in most cases, the teen can only stand so much clutter themselves and become desperate to see the floor once again. This is especially true if the rest of the home is clean and tidy.

So, take heart, oh parent. Pick your battles and leave the rest to destiny. Enjoy your children. Envision them as adults in a few years. Ask yourself, "What do I want my child to remember most about his or her childhood?"

One word of caution: What you harp on now just might stick, but won't take root until your children become adults. Then, as old age sets in on you, your children will seem to become as touchy or touchier than you were about certain issues. You know the adage: like father, like son; like mother, like daughter.

This issue crops up in the strangest places, like behind the wheel of the car. You never had a problem driving, but now you visit your adult children, and they think you are going to kill them if they don't inspect and direct your driving habits. Or, in my case, I now have a daughter who makes certain that guests in her home do not rock back on the kitchen or dining room chairs.

Such a pity. It looked so relaxing when Kelly did it as a child. But, you see, we had to teach her proper manners. Now I am forced into submission to the very thing we cured her of years ago. At least she doesn't fasten the chairs to the floor when she sees me coming.

As I think back to our children's childhood, I smile and think of all the wonderful lessons they taught me about raising children. They often had a smile accompanied by a malicious intent. You can be certain I had fun trying to figure out how to get the best of them when the history of my own childhood would have dictated that I should be a mean disciplinarian. Joy comes in creativity and in having a child grow into an adult believing in you and giving you value, not only for who you are, but for the pleasant memories about disciplining without malice.

REVIEW

- If appropriate, use the same strategy on your children as they use on you. They will be sure to understand it better.

- Any question you ask a child must be clearly thought out with the correct use of words so the truth will be drawn out.

- Do not tell a child all his options or consequences at the beginning. You just might want to change your mind before it's all over.

- A child's urgency should be weighed as to its importance.

- Cornering or boxing a child in with no way of escape or no ability to save face is not wise and will cause you to lose more than what you hoped to gain.

- Pick your battle. If it isn't worth the fight, leave it for maturity or for their marriage partner to resolve.

CHAPTER 13

Boundaries for your empty nest

Sitting at the table of your offspring occasionally makes for better relationships than if they sit at yours indefinitely.

—Tom Sanford

We were not only good friends but also neighbors. Irv was a good 30 years older than I but was still very active. As a matter of fact, when most people have retired, or are at least thinking about it, Irv, at age 70, was buying a restaurant and looking forward to his third career. Irv had started out as a pharmacist, then bought a gas and oil distributorship. In less than a year after he sold his business, he was buying another one.

There is something else I must tell you about Irv. He had recently married a 55- year-old woman with two adult children. Irv's first wife had passed away five years before and for several years he had kept her ashes on the fireplace mantel in his living room. I didn't realize they were there until one day he said to me, "Tom, it's time for me to get on with my life. Could you take me for a little plane ride so I can scatter my wife's ashes over the mountains?"

I had never done that before and expressed some concerns – like blasting the paint off the side of the plane as he scattered the ashes. After all, when you rent a plane they expect it to come back with as much paint as it had on when it left. I could just see the sandblasted horizontal stabilizer in my mind. But, not wanting to disappoint him, I took the chance.

Just as confident as he was about closing that chapter in his life he was equally confident that his new marriage would be great. She was "young and pretty," so he declared. "And the boys could help with keeping the yard up."

"Young!" I thought to myself. "Why, she's almost old enough to be my mother. Besides she has a 30-year-old son." Boy, did I ever get a good lesson in perspective.

One thing Irv had never done before was come to my office for any reason. But, six months into his new marriage he showed up – unannounced and uninvited. He didn't even wait for a greeting or an invitation to have a seat. He just walked in and plopped himself down in the chair nearest my desk. As a matter of fact, he didn't even take the time for pleasant formalities. He was on a mission and I could tell it. His jaw was set and his eyes had that far off look.

"Tom," he began, "have you ever had a passion to go to the remotest place in Montana, find an abandoned logging road, drive to the very end, build a cabin and just live there in total solitude until you died?"

"Irv, you're having marriage problems aren't you?" I blurted out so spontaneously that it surprised even me. I could tell a storm was brewing on the horizon of the tranquil existence he once enjoyed. His life and his home were no longer his own. The wife of his youth was gone, and out of loneliness he had taken the risk of loving again.

With a sigh that told me he was relieved at not having to explain the reason for his visit, he leaned forward and told me a story I have heard all too often – before and since.

Irv explained he had tried to set down some ground rules and establish chores for each of his new young residents with absolutely no success. He couldn't even get the 30 year old motivated to get a job. "What's worse," he moaned, "is my wife has her suitcase packed and declares, in no uncertain terms, she is moving out if I kick him out."

"So, you feel the only way out of this predicament is to run away yourself and leave no forwarding address. Is that correct?" I asked. He nodded in a defeated gesture.

"Okay, Irv," I said with a bit of enthusiasm that shocked him. "You're not leaving until you get the packrats out of your lower level. You'll enjoy your trip to Montana much better. First, consider how old you will be when the 30-year-old free loader is 50. Can you imagine a 90-year-old man supporting a 50 year old?" He shook his head with a bit of surprise.

"You are going to have to take a risk," I encouraged. "But it is a risk that I think will come out to your good. Here it is: Forget your wife's threat and quit looking at her packed suitcase. That is only a ploy to force you into submission. But if she does leave, pray she takes her kids with her. As unorthodox as that may sound, Irv, you have to do something now or you will never regain control."

With that introduction I told Irv his only compromise should be to rent an apartment for two months for his stepson, move him out and announce that he has two months to get a job because he isn't moving back home and you aren't paying any more rent.

"Once you have the 30 year old tamed, then you can deal with the 20 year old. But he's a bit different because he's in school."

Irv walked out of my office with determination. "After all," he confessed, "I don't think I could stand all that cold and snow in Montana."

I didn't see Irv for another six months and was a bit nervous about calling his house – afraid that all might have failed and he had left for Montana. But one day, to my

surprise, he walked into my office – again totally
unannounced. "I did it and it worked," he smiled.

"What about your wife's suitcase?" I asked quizzically.

"Oh, that. Once she knew I meant business she
unpacked it and I haven't heard anymore about it."

"And the son?"

"Ah, he got a job within two weeks after I moved him
out. And, he moved into another apartment. It seems he
didn't like my selection," he laughed a bit sarcastically.

With the number of adult children moving back home
due to unemployment, divorce, finances, or one of several
other reasons, it is time parents take charge of their own
home. If you don't, these adult children will be harder to
get rid of later on and perhaps cost you plenty of stress,
money and sleep during what you thought were going to be
your peaceful retirement years.

Here are a couple examples of heartbreaking situations
that should be a warning sign to all of us. One couple
mortgaged their home to keep their *resident* son from going
bankrupt. It seems he promised he would pay them back as
soon as he got back on his feet. It just so happened that he
never considered himself "back on his feet". Even a couple
years later when he was experiencing quite an affluent
lifestyle with absolutely no housing costs, Mom and Dad
had grown accustomed to him living at home. Ironically,
they would wake up in the mornings angry and didn't
know why.

Number one mistake: not charging their son rent. After
all, "He is our son. He might be offended if we suggest he
pay rent." Number two mistake: not having their son sign a
note for repayment. It was merely a word of mouth

agreement. Their son concluded he was unable to pay them back until he had paid off all his toys. Maybe he figured if he waited long enough he would collect on his inheritance and save on the pain of paying them back.

In another case the parents had the last laugh. In their will they stated that all their assets, upon their death, would be split between all of their children except one. The will declared no money or anything else would go to this particular son because, "we have given him more than his share of the inheritance during our lifetime." It's too bad they didn't have the nerve when they were still alive to tell him they weren't going to give him any more money.

The one thing more tragic than loaning your children money, which you might never see again, is to have them nickel and dime you to death.

How about another couple who had to sell the home they had lived in for 40 years and move into a one-bedroom house just for peace and quiet. As much as they loved their daughter, son-in-law, and three grandchildren, the house was getting smaller every day.

Far more often than we'd like to think, adult children are having their own children, moving in with their parents for a period of time and then walking away and leaving the grandchildren. I don't know of any grandparents who would abandon their grandchildren because of the inappropriate lifestyle of their son or daughter. We need to commend those who graciously raise a second family in their retirement years.

So, let's talk about ways you can maintain control, protect your finances and assure yourself you won't get to be 80 while still supporting a 40 year old. It might be tough at first, but you can handle it. It's like going out deep sea fishing. You have to endure the breakers getting out of port before the waters begin to calm down. And if your entire fishing trip is stormy, make it back to port and check in with a professional on some sound advice before you try the breakers again.

Regardless of whether your child never leaves home because of attending college locally or he or she returns home after college; whether your child never goes to college or a host of other causes – don't let them live at home without it costing them something! It's simply a matter of responsibility, accountability, respect, and continuing the development of integrity in your child through this stage in his or her life.

Our son decided it was cheaper to stay at home while going to college. While we were honored that he wanted to stay at home, I made sure, early in his final year, to let him know I would give him three months after college before rent and boarding charges would be assessed. Before you begin to think this is cruel and unusual punishment, keep reading before you pass final judgment.

Remember my words just a bit earlier about responsibility, accountability, respect and integrity? I merely asked for a reasonable percentage of his income for housing and an additional percentage for food. Plus, if he was going to use my car, he had to return it with as much gas as was in it prior to him borrowing it.

Oh, one more thing – he was responsible for the oil changes. He chose to take the cheaper option and serviced the car himself. For those who are not mechanically inclined it is best to insist on a reputable service company to do that.

Knowing ahead of time what was expected of him helped avoid the possibility of a hostile environment; he knew the expectations and limitations. He also agreed that the percentages were reasonable and fair. Being the resourceful person that he is, he wanted to make certain my percentages were indeed fair. So, one day at the table he proposed that he should not pay any more for rent, percentage wise, than what my house payment was costing me. I thought that was fair so I let him get his calculator and figure out my income/housing ratio as well. After a few moments of calculating, he promptly closed the calculator and continued eating without saying another word.

"What's the matter," I asked with a grin, "Is the deal off?"

It wasn't until he was almost finished eating that he could muster the courage to confess that I was paying a good seven percent more of my income on housing than the percentage I was charging him. He was now eager to keep the rent agreement as I had originally proposed.

If your adult child has no job, you can still assess his or her unemployment payments. But, if there is no income whatsoever, you can always establish values for work that needs to be done around the house. After all, why should you be mowing the lawn and weeding the garden when your able bodied offspring is inside watching TV without seemingly a worry about his or her future.

Consider the wonderful possibilities of saving money with your return nester. You could even cancel some of your services since you now have a built-in housekeeper. What's nice about this idea is you already know them.

Therefore, their references are easily accessible – day or night. What I am saying is this: Before they walk in the front door and put their suitcases down, consider your history with them and their amiability. If they left in hostility and are returning with unresolved issues, ask yourself this question, "If I was hiring – would I give this person a second thought?"

"But wait!" you shout. "This is my child. I can't just turn them away." Maybe not, but you still don't have to let them disrupt your life by charging back home and ruling the roost. It would be far cheaper, emotionally and financially, to do what Irv did. Rent them an apartment for a short time. And, if you find it difficult to say no to an overbearing, dominant adult child, this would be a wonderful time to change the locks and go on vacation. While you're gone see if you can find a class on codependency so you can establish and maintain some healthy boundaries.

The biggest challenge will be to set boundaries that you might not have set when they were young. This is the time that all your skills will be called into action. It's the time to be sure you are in control. Giving in or feeling sorry for one who intentionally or unintentionally wants to cash in his or her inheritance early will only lead to discord or unhappiness as time goes on. You might feel the need to rescue one who has squandered both his life and resources, but the other siblings are going to begin to resent you in the process.

The difference between you and the prodigal's father in Luke 15 is that while he welcomed the wayward son back home, he respected the older son's inheritance and did not offer to take more away from him in order to support the younger. Further, the younger son knew, before he even came home, that the consequence for being foolish and squandering his resources was that he would have to resort to manual labor where before he lived a life of luxury. He knew this so well that he had it rehearsed so he wouldn't have to waste his father's breath.

By now you are probably thinking, "At what age is it appropriate to practice this concept?" There are some people who would like me to suggest a definite age they can set as their goal. It's not that easy.

The principle I use is: Whenever your offspring are finished with school, regardless of whether they are 16 or 23, they should begin to assume responsibility for their own upkeep. Don't be suckered into the excuse, "I can't find a job." If they have dropped out of school, accountability might just inspire them to go back to school so they can pay their bills.

Be careful of some children who become *career* students. In those cases, I would tie this principle to either the number of years in college or a degree. I would also consider their adult lifestyle or marital status. Marriage should be a clue to you that they want to establish a home of their own. Just don't let them make it yours.

Another consideration is whether your adult child has any physical or mental challenges that would preclude their ability for some type of employment.

Regardless of the circumstances and considerations, the point is this: Adult children are adults, not *children*, who should be allowed to grow up and be independent. It is better for everyone concerned that they accept responsibility for themselves. This cannot help but result in positive self-esteem and the broadening of their horizons.

The other side of the coin is you, as parents, have earned the right to pursue your own lives after *serving* and, in many cases, sacrificing for your children.

There is nothing wrong with being honest with your adult child and saying, "I love you, but I won't support you. You have what it takes to make a life of your own." Don't even discuss whether you can afford it or not. That is not the issue. The issue is making sure your adult child assumes responsibility for his or her own actions.

REVIEW

- Any offspring who drops out of school or graduates should pay rent if they wish to live at home.

- No loans should be by handshake or verbal agreement. A legal note should be signed by your son or daughter.

- To be fair to all your children, do not indulge one over the others. If you only have one child, make him wait for his inheritance just in case you need it yourself.

- If you don't have the nerve to say no to an adult child, seek professional help.

- Helping an adult child to be independent will improve his or her responsibility, accountability, respect and integrity.

- The absence of a job should never be an excuse for lack of accountability.

- Some situations require more strategic planning than others, but you can succeed with prayer and consultation.

- Saying "no" is not synonymous with not loving.

SUMMARY

I hope this book has captivated an interest in you to do something special with your children beyond the thoughtless and often meaningless discipline we often see around us. It should be your desire to create in your child a life that wakes up every morning with the joy of another day. They should have the spirit of wonderment as to what Mom or Dad are going to do to surprise them – even when they are behaving badly.

There are a couple recurring cautions in every family's life that bear thoughtful consideration as you look towards the future of your parenting. They are as follows:

1. No restraint on your children now means no constraint on their part when they grow into their teen years.

2. Don't expect your child to know as much as you, or behave like you. On the other hand, maybe the child does behave like you, and that is what might bother you about him or her.

In your child is the making of royalty. For, indeed, they are the *children of God*.

I am recapturing the high points of the book in this section for a quick review. If your child challenges you, in any way, you can stare them in the eyes and say, "Just a minute, I am new at this. Let me check and see what I am supposed to do next." Then run to your closet and review the basics in this summary.

Begin your consistency and love attack on your child by remembering the quote by St. Francis of Assisi: "Start by doing what is necessary, then do what is possible. Suddenly you are doing the impossible."

CHAPTER ONE

- Good parenting takes cooperative support from both parents.

- Demeaning behavior or words to or about a child are counterproductive, wrong and abusive.

- Do not bring into your parenting agendas anything from your own childhood that is demeaning or unhealthy.

- Obnoxious habits you developed to control your child will come back to spite you as your children grow into adulthood.

- Make certain all discipline is safe.

- Do not embarrass a child. He will find it difficult to forget or forgive.

CHAPTER TWO

- Anger is not a reliable or appropriate way to discipline. It only lends itself to provoking anger in the child.

- If you wish your children to love and respect you when they become adults – demonstrate love and respect for them as children.

- God's rules don't change and neither should ours.

- There are consequences for our behavior.

- Children have value and need to be treated as such.

CHAPTER THREE

- The excitement of childhood should not be interrupted by the fear of reprisal.

- Children should learn to fear dangers but never have to fear their parents.

- Children will subconsciously do things to protect themselves from known predators.

- Believing in a child furthers their growth much faster than disapproving of their behavior.

CHAPTER FOUR

- Humor without sarcasm works wonders when nothing else will.

- A smile will do two things in a tense situation: 1. It will disarm or reduce tension, and will catch the verbal assailant off guard. 2. It will buy you time to think rather than react.

- Hyperboles are an effective tool in dealing with teens. As a matter of fact, it is so effective that your teens have been using it, or soon will be using it, on you.

CHAPTER FIVE

- Children generally lay awake at night figuring out how to outsmart their parents. Parents should do the same on behalf of their children. The problem is – children don't have to stay awake very long compared to the parents.

- Creativity is essential in discipline if one wishes to go beyond the lazy practice of getting angry and yelling and, perhaps, spanking.

- Do not presuppose you can manage your child just because you are older, wiser, bigger, and their parent.

CHAPTER SIX

- If it isn't your fault, why get upset? If it is your fault, why blame the child?

- Change the mistakes your child makes into "teachable moments" rather than a time to release your own pent up frustrations.

- Getting even is not a right a parent has.

- Improve relationships by giving your child the right to respond and a chance to fix the problem.

- Consequences do not require emotional involvement on the part of the parent.

- Be certain you understand clearly the difference between rights and privileges.

- If you didn't cause it, why fix it? That is the responsibility of the one who broke it.

- Compromise is a good thing. The goal is generally reached sooner and easier.

CHAPTER SEVEN

- If logic doesn't work, don't use it.

- Being right is not as important as being happy. If someone wants to prove you wrong, they will.

- Logic should never be the point of an argument. Love and forgiveness should be the focal points.

CHAPTER EIGHT

- Teaching children is far better than just making them watch.

- Encourage your child to become what they want to be rather than what you expect of them.

- Help strengthen your child's interests even if they aren't your interests. Find a mentor if necessary. This will go a long way in reducing a teen's interest in drugs, crime and poor friends.

CHAPTER NINE

- Enforceable rules must be fair.

- Being fair is not synonymous with being equal.

- Insisting on anything you cannot or will not enforce is a dead-end street. "Say what you mean, mean what you say and don't be mean about it."

- There must be a good reason for a rule. Regardless of how good you think a rule is, if you don't follow through with it, then eliminate it.

- Delaying any consequence is not healthy. It merely breeds contempt.

- Regardless of what names a child calls you, what they say about your lineage, looks, intelligence, or body odor – stay focused on the issue. Later, when the issue has been resolved you can research the validity of those charges.

CHAPTER TEN

- Everyone deserves a compliment which should precede any talk of discipline.

- A good rule of thumb is: If a teen is bigger or faster than you, don't use force. It is a sure way to lose.

- Strategize, strategize, strategize.

- You must ask yourself; "Is this about my own personal pride or prejudice, or is it about my child's well being?" If it is the former you should think twice before you *pick the fight.*

CHAPTER ELEVEN

- Wrong assumptions cripple relationships and communication.

- If you are going to assume anything, assume the best rather than the worst.

- The key is – never assume anything.

CHAPTER TWELVE

- If appropriate, use the same strategy on your children as they use on you. They will be sure to understand it better.

- Any question you ask a child must be clearly thought out with the correct use of words so the truth will be drawn out.

- Do not tell a child all his options or consequences at the beginning.

- A child's urgency should be weighed as to its importance.

- Cornering or boxing a child in with no way of escape or no ability to *save face* is not wise and will cause you to lose more than what you hoped to gain.

- Pick your battle. If it isn't worth the fight, leave it for maturity or for their marriage partner to resolve.

CHAPTER THIRTEEN

- Any offspring who drops out of school or graduates should pay rent if they wish to live at home.

- No loans should be by handshake or verbal agreement. A legal note should be signed by your son or daughter.

- To be fair to all your children, do not indulge one over the others. If you only have one child, make him wait for his inheritance just in case you need it yourself.

- If you don't have the nerve to say no to an adult child, seek professional help.

- Helping an adult child to be independent will improve his or her responsibility, accountability, respect and integrity.

- The absence of a job should never be an excuse for lack of accountability.

- Some situations require more strategic planning than others, but you can succeed with prayer and consultation.

- Saying "no" is not synonymous with not loving.

IF PARENTING IS A THREE RING CIRCUS, HOW COME I'M NOT THE RINGMASTER?

POSTSCRIPT

I'm Tom's son, Craig, and growing up with a father who was creative was not an easy task. As a matter of fact, as a teen, I thought it was a real pain. After all, you don't get what you want when you want it. I remember being a bit jealous of my friends who got their *needs* met on a regular basis.

Maybe it's because I started life on the *wrong foot*. At a very early age I can remember tearing apart my mom's vacuum sweeper. I also tried to fix a defunct alarm clock, only to have my dad declare it *dead on arrival* and throw it away.

When I wanted a boat to go fishing, my dad said, "You're my boat." I didn't realize at the time that meant he couldn't afford one. Learning some strategies from my childhood friends, I decided to persist in my *need* for a boat. My dad finally gave in and said, "Okay, you can have a boat."

I knew it! I knew it! My friends were right. Persist and beg long enough and your parents will tire of listening to you and get you what you want.

He told me, since I was so persistent, we could go get the boat right then. So, we got in our pickup and headed off to buy my long dreamed for boat.

It wasn't long before we pulled into a lumberyard. I asked my dad why we were stopping at a lumberyard. He insisted it wasn't a lumberyard, but rather a shipyard. All of a sudden I was struck with the reality that I wasn't going to get a boat the easy way. We bought a couple sheets of plywood, some two by twos, screws, Styrofoam, caulking and some special marine paint.

Needless to say, it took me a month to build my boat. My dad did help, but I learned all about how to get plywood to curve, why it was important to caulk the seams, and the importance of the special paint.

See what I mean about living with a creative father? You just might get what you want, but you sure are going to have to work for it.

In my late teens I was feeling kind of down on myself thinking I had no real talent. My dad tried to assure me I had lots of talent. When I kept insisting that there was nothing I was really good at, he grew silent. A couple hours later he asked me if I would mind going for a ride with him. I agreed. That was a big mistake.

We drove to an auto wrecking yard that sold rebuildable automobiles. We wandered through the rebuild lot. He got me again. There, sitting beside each other, were two vehicles – same model and same year. One had a good body, but was only a two-wheel drive with a bad engine. The other had been rolled over. The body was pretty well crushed. However, it was a four-wheel drive with low mileage and a good frame.

We bought both and had them hauled home where I started switching bodies. A few weeks later I had a great four-wheel SUV that I was able to sell easily and make a profit.

I really don't like auto mechanics, and I could never see myself being a professional mechanic. However, I found a talent that I wanted to deny even though it gave me a sense of pride and value and that saves me a bunch of money when my own vehicle needs repairing.

Here's an important lesson I learned that I want to pass on. When I would work on a car, I wanted my repair to be clean, strong and durable. In an effort to be certain the bolts or nuts would not come loose, I would tighten everything as tight as I could. Sometimes, before I knew it, I had tightened a bolt too tight and would break something.

I always meant well, but when I broke something by over tightening it, the cost and time to fix it climbed exponentially. To calm my frustrations at those times, my father would teach me to feel the turn of the wrench to know when enough was enough. I learned that each nut and bolt is engineered to accept certain forces or stresses. That is known as the torque value. If you exceed this value things will break.

"Torqued off" is a phrase we often hear. This is when people have reached their limit or breaking point. If you apply the above analogy, you can make a discipline parallel. This concept of knowing the limits of discipline is of great importance. We all have a significant influence on others – especially children. Therefore, you must know the limits. In a desire to make the child strong and disciplined, you can inflict more damage than correction. Just like the nut-and-bolt analogy, your cost and time to repair the relationship has just risen.

That's why my father's book is so important. It gives you a way of feeling when enough is enough, and how to avoid the breakdowns in the first place. I hope the firsthand wisdom my father has put in this book will help you become a more effective parent.

It's never too late to learn. My parents' skills in learning the limits of fair and effective discipline was not an overnight experience. My sister, Kelly, and I had a lot of training to do. Every parent needs to understand something my parents mastered. That is how to grow and flex with the variability in each child.

Thanks Dad and Mom for learning your limits and mine – from the firm hand on the shoulder to the gentle guiding touch.

Craig Sanford

Project PATCH (Planned Assistance for Troubled CHildren) was founded in 1984 by Tom and Bonnie Sanford. The initial purpose of the program was to provide specialized resources for "at risk" children from birth to 18. In 1989 Project PATCH was able to acquire property in Garden Valley, Idaho, to begin a residential year-round program. At that time PATCH no longer continued serving as a foster care program.

By 1993 Project PATCH Youth Ranch was licensed by the Idaho Department of Health and Welfare. Sixteen young men and 16 young ladies between the ages of 12 and 18 make up the nucleus of the facility. To provide for optimal care for these youth, PATCH employs more than 40 staff, which includes four professional counselors.

Realizing that a spiritual dynamic is important to a therapy program which expects to have a lasting impact on the lives of young people, Project PATCH also employs a full-time chaplain.

In addition to its licensure with the State of Idaho for its residential program, Project PATCH's wilderness program is also approved and licensed by the State of Idaho.

The school that Project PATCH operates on its campus is accredited as an alternative school through the Idaho Department of Education and the Northwest Association of Accredited Schools. It also has received full facility accreditation through Joint Commission on Accreditation of Healthcare Organizations (JCAHO), for both the residential and wilderness programs.

MISSION STATEMENT

Project PATCH is passionately committed to reaching out to young people throughout the United States and Canada who are at risk and help them realize their self-worth, potential and the significance of God's love to them.

VISION STATEMENT

FOR PROJECT PATCH: *To be the recognized leader in providing specialized services to adolescents in crises.*

FOR THE STAFF: *To portray excellence in teamwork, relationships and performance.*

PROJECT PATCH BELIEVES...

…in the uniqueness and value of every young person, including those who have become troubled.

…that every at-risk youth deserves an environment within which they can find restoration and healing

…in the necessity of a program dedicated to the individual needs of each resident.

…in the necessity of teaching responsible living to every troubled youth.

…healthy relationships between adults and youth are indispensable for at-risk youth to achieve healing.

…assisting troubled youth in cultivating a relationship with Jesus Christ is the most effective means of achieving healing.

Information about Project PATCH can be obtained on the internet at **www.projectpatch.org** or by calling **503-653-8086**.

Additional Resources

CREATIVE PARENTING SEMINARS

The author, Tom Sanford, is available for speaking appointments sharing, in his captivating and humorous way, creative discipline techniques. These seminars include numerous first-hand illustrations not included in the book as well as the tried and true techniques you've just read about.

For available dates and fees contact Project PATCH at (503) 653-8086 or patch@projectpatch.org.

ADDITIONAL BOOK COPIES

Purchase additional copies of "If Parenting is a Three Ring Circus, How Come I'm Not the Ringmaster" for family and friends. This book is also a great gift for teachers, youth leaders and new parents, to be given at baby showers or dedications. Bulk rates are also available for purchases of 50 or more.

Quantity: _____ x $15.49 per book (includes shipping & handling)

Total: $_____

Ship to:

_____
Name

_____
Address

_____

(____) _____   _____
Phone   E-mail

Send check for total, along with shipping information, to:
Project PATCH
Attn: Book Orders
13455 SE 97th Avenue
Clackamas, OR 97015

Call (503) 653-8086 for bulk rates.

INVEST IN THE FUTURE OF TROUBLED YOUTH

Proceeds from the sale of this book go to support the work of Project PATCH. If you would like to invest in the future of troubled youth, Tom Sanford would love to talk to you. Project PATCH, and the kids it helps, depend on private and corporate donations from people like you.

I would like to support Project PATCH **each month** by sending a gift of:
☐ $500   ☐ $250   ☐ $100   ☐ $50   ☐ other $_____
I am sending a one-time gift of $_____

Please charge $_____ to my
☐ Visa   ☐ MasterCard   Exp. Date_____

Card # _____

Signature _____

_____
Name

_____
Address

_____

(___) _____   _____

Contributions can be sent to:
Project PATCH
13455 SE 97th Avenue
Clackamas, OR 97015

Online contributions
can be made at:
www.projectpatch.org.

All gifts are tax deductible.

About the Author

Tom Sanford graduated from Andrews University with a bachelor's degree in theology. He served as pastor in both Montana and Oregon for 15 years.

During those years he negotiated with juvenile courts to provide alternatives to detention for numerous young people.

He served as a member and chairperson of the Hood River County Juvenile Services Commission in Hood River, Oregon. He and his wife, Bonnie, have kept over 100 children in their home over the course of 30 years. He also served as Chaplain and Search Pilot for the Civil Air Patrol for nearly 20 years.

He is the Founder and Director of Project PATCH, an accredited residential program for at-risk youth. PATCH began in 1984 and presently serves youth from 12-17 years of age.